Dedication

Dedicated to all the officers who drive those black and white patrol cars, therefore, I chose black and white for the cover of this book.

POLICING
THE OLD MOJAVE DESERT

L.A. "Buzz" Banks
Sgt. #436, Retired
California Highway Patrol

4

This republication is in memory of my dad.
1913-1999

We have received many requests for replacement and gift
copies of the first sold-out self-published edition. This
speaks of many treasured books.
So more can share....

TABLE OF CONTENTS

Chapter
1. Traffic Laws Come to the Mojave Desert 9
2. Guns, Drugs, and Farewell, Part One 19
2. Guns, Drugs, and Farewell, Part Two 25
2. Doc; A Very Complex Man, Part Three 23
3. Victorville As It Was 31
4. My First Close Call 38
5. One Way to Get the Other's Attention 42
6. If Only That Old Sheriff's Office Could Talk 46
7. Deserts Seem to Develop Unusual People 53
8. Crossing the Mojave Desert Had Its Problems 58
9. Judge Roy Bean Would Have Loved Victorville 64
10. To Bathe Or Not To Bathe 69
11. When California Was Invaded from the Midwest 74
12. Carl McNew; Victorville's Quiet Pistolero 79
13. Hard Work and Hard Rocks 84
14. Pimps, Prosties, and Politicians 89
15. Victorville, A Wartime Peyton Place 93
16. Victorville, A Tough Little Town 95
17. A Police Officer's Job is Like No Other 101
18. Death on Summer Day 106
19. We Lose A Fine Young Officer 110
20. Luck Still Controls Whether We Live or Die 114
21. Young Officers Can Be Too Young 119
22. When Luck Runs Out on Old U.S. Highway #66 121
23. The Agony Of Fearing the Worst 124
24. Spies in the Outhouse 127
25. Who Dat Say Who Dat When I Say Who Dat? 130
26. Sure And It's Not What I Meant 132
27. Onlookers Can Be Problems 134
28. Alibis 136
29. Different People, Different Behavior 138
30. The Inner Fear Shared By Officers' Wives 142
31. Uncommon Drunks I Have Met – And Had to Arrest 148
32. Laws of Today Do Not Fit The Problems 153

FOREWARD

For any inaccuracies contained in these stories I wish at this time to offer my apologies. Wherever reasonably possible, I have verified the substance of all of them.

All written history has many wrong claims, some inadvertent, some careless and some have been deliberate. Winners write the historical books, not the losers.

Nor are old newspaper articles to be trusted completely for reference material. Such news usually is only partially correct. So please bear with me, and enjoy it, knowing that nothing has been exaggerated nor distorted for any reason. It has been great simply to recall some of my experiences, and a few which I saw as they happened, or learned from talking with the lawmen involved.

I am grateful, too, that I was lucky to serve as a law officer during the best period we will ever see, and lucky that I was assigned to the Mojave Desert and the little town that was Victorville.

Also, a special thanks goes to a good friend and famous western artist, Bill Bender, for the sketch shown on the back cover, to illustrate an actual occurrence which is described in the book.

**One way to get the other's attention.
Sketch by Bill Bender.**

Walt Terry radioing to his office.

CHAPTER ONE
TRAFFIC LAWS COME TO THE MOJAVE DESERT

You never can find a cop when you need one! How often has this remark been grumbled? Well, in the case of the Mojave Desert there were almost no cops. Historians write about the old days, but they never mention any police, unless a murder has been committed and deputies are sent out from San Bernardino to investigate the crime.

Lawmen in the desert were elected as constables, men who had no law training and had other jobs.

In 1929 the California Highway Patrol was established, employing a few hundred men who up to then had been county traffic cops, but there was no state traffic law, only local laws until 1935 when the State Legislature passed the Calif. Vehicle Code. Now it was time to look for men such as Walt Terry to build up the Patrol in order to do a real job of policing every mile of roads and highways in California.

It was an exceptional person who joined the Patrol in 1937 at a time when law enforcement was changing but nobody could foresee its direction. To make matters tougher, he was assigned as one of two resident officers in Barstow, some eighty miles from the squad office in San Bernardino, where once in a great while a sergeant might come out on a motorcycle for a few hours. Just about everything was done on motors in those days.

Here we have a rookie officer with almost no academy training, no experience and no guidance sent out to patrol an area from the Kern County line to the Colorado River and from Inyo County south to an imaginary line east and west across the lower

Mojave desert. The total area exceeded ten thousand square miles.

Just imagine a young man given so much responsibility! But Walt was equal to it. He realized he needed all the cooperation he could get, so he made friends everywhere, from businessmen to railroad workers, from one end of his enormous beat to the other.

There were no radios. Communication was by way of at most a dozen phones along the roads across the desert. All the owners were asked to call in emergency requests to a pharmacy in Barstow owned by George Cunningham. There was no manned sheriff's office to take calls.

George or an employee would then turn on a flashing light or set out a flag, thus informing Walt of an emergency somewhere along his beat. Sometimes the message would be relayed to the few service stations because Walt would always stop for a visit and to see if he had any calls. This was necessary as Terry might be away all day.

Walt had established a communications system where none had existed, and he did it because folks wanted to help him. Even when the CHP installed radios they were too weak to do much good, and it took a long while before there were enough repeaters to cover the desert.

For several years the sixty-one Harley was the CHP motorcycle, agile and fast. When the "seventy-fours" came into use it was because they were more powerful and could haul the big, clumsy radios with the vacuum tubes. Either way, they were all we had. Imagine being called out of a warm bed on a freezing winter night around midnight to respond to a traffic collision about a hundred miles away. Imagine bundling up in warm clothes, then working up a sweat trying to kickstart

a cold and obstinate motor! Then the gas tank had
to be filled on the way out and again on the way
back. Sometimes another accident might occur
another hundred miles away. No wonder Terry
developed a mustache; it was too many hours
between a cleanup and a shave.

But Walt was equal to it, rugged and tough.
He was sometimes referred to as the "Iron Man of
the Desert" because he never complained and
never took a day of sick leave in his entire career.
Sometimes, on those long cold rides back to
Barstow it wouldn't be unusual to park the bike,
gather up a little dry brush, start a fire to squat
beside and thaw out, then climb aboard and ride
some more.

When finally Sacramento sent down a car it
had no heater. The high brass thought the desert
was next door to Hades! A Coleman lantern rigged
up so it wouldn't give off light did just fine to keep
the patrol car warm.

All in all, it was a job of improvising, to make
do with whatever was at hand. It supposedly was a
six day per week job, not five, but also it required
being on call twenty-four hours per day, seven days
per week. Walt loved to hunt and fish, but if he
planned to be gone, he had to make arrangements
for someone to stand by for him.

As time went by the Barstow resident post
increased in numbers, becoming a sub-station with
a sergeant and eventually it achieved full status as
a squad area, along with a captain in charge.

Through all these changes Walt remained
Walt, even after he made sergeant.

In early 1960 the CHP tried out the use of
fixed wing aircraft for patrol duty, with Terry
serving as the field supervisor, which literally put
him in charge of the operation.

Terry would retire in 1965, then join the San Bernardino County Coroner's office as a deputy coroner, again covering the entire desert he had served so well in his days with the CHP. He stayed with this job of for several years, using his own pickup instead of a county car. Behind the cab he had stuck a shovel on one side and a broom on the other. When asked why, he would respond with a remark to the effect that he had to dig in for the facts, then clean up the mess.

Everything lawmen had to work with in those days is gone today. Even the "six-gun" has given way to the automatic with its greater fire power. Newcomers have no idea how it was.

In 1947 Walt went to the little mining town of Red Mountain at the northwest corner of San Bernardino County to help with the traffic expected because the folks there had decided to put on a rodeo.

Traffic and the crowd were even more than anticipated, and Terry was the only uniformed lawman there. The deputies always dressed like cowboys because their county still prided itself as being "cow county." They weren't much help with crowd control and asked Walt to help out.

He couldn't do much on foot, and the patrol car was no better. Someone fixed him up with a saddled horse and he was in business. Sadly, the horse was not shod for pavement and it slipped, landing on Walt's hip, breaking it.

Walt went to the hospital, and two officers were sent to bring in his patrol car. But now there was a dilemma. Would Sacramento refuse to believe he was entitled to 4800 time (off, due to job related injury) or would they say he had no business riding a horse and was simply goofing off?

Well, headquarters accepted it and Terry didn't have to use up his sick leave. At the time everyone was happy that things had turned out well, but I have often wondered if he sustained a deeper injury which turned him into such a pathetic invalid in his last years. Walt never complained even during the few times he was suffering with a severe cold or the flu. He had a reputation to maintain as the "Iron Man!" In my view he should have had many more active years.

Terry was the kind of man who was always ready to go wherever he felt he could help others, and because he was good at it he was allowed full freedom to move about almost at will, and none of the subsequent squad commanders would deny him whatever he felt he should do.

He was a brand new officer when the heavy snows of 1937 buried most of San Bernardino County and the desert under several feet of snow. Walt was out there on a motorcycle as soon as the roads were opened, at great risk to himself, to help stranded ranchers and others. Fortunately, the snow was very wet and there was little wind, so no drifts piled up. It stayed cold and the mountains gained more of the white stuff.

Winter wasn't over when a warm rain of several days duration deluged the land, melting all that snow, causing the most disastrous floods seen in California for nearly a century. Water poured down the Mojave River all the way to Baker and beyond, filling the entire basin and five dry lakes along the way. Roads were washed out, ranches were cut off from all escape, and vehicles were stranded everywhere.

Again Walt was there to work with the highway foreman to locate the worst problems needing repairs, get tow trucks to the many stalled vehicles, and locate isolated ranches. What a job for a brand new officer, alone and on his own!

An even worse storm and freeze hit in 1949, with forty inches of snow in the hills only a few miles from Needles, California. Even worse, it was a dry snow, accompanied by winds of forty miles per hour which caused drifts thirty to forty feet deep. So many ranch houses were completely buried the first flyers to make reconnaissance flights thought the land below them was an empty desert.

For days nothing could move. Many cattle died, some frozen to death while standing upright. Into this tragedy went Terry, literally disappearing for three days. Our radio repeaters were out for most of the time, but somehow he was the one who was able to relay the information that the military was needed to airlift hay to the stranded cattle and bring in "weasels" which were the only vehicles capable of getting through to the ranchers.

Throughout, Walt couldn't have used the patrol car very much, but with his knowledge of the desert, and because he was a friend to every soul who lived in it, somehow he managed to eat a few meals, sleep a few hours, and get a little gasoline when needed. He never had much to say about those three days. Again, he had been the Iron Man.

Among his may friends were Rex Bell and Clara Bow, the former movie cowboy and the "It" girl of the twenties. Rex had become governor of Nevada and their ranch was just inside that state line, not far from Whiskey Pete's.

Occasionally Walt would stop for a short visit when he patrolled to the line. He told of a desert Bighorn sheep which had grown too old to forage and was being fed at the ranch out of kindness. He said to watch out for it as it just loved to catch someone in a bent over position. At that moment the sheep seemed to think it was a goat, and took appropriate action.

There really was a bootlegger known as "Whiskey Pete" who made and sold his wares near the California-Nevada state line. He had passed on before prohibition ended and before Terry came along, but an entrepreneur of sorts put up a shack at the edge of the dry lake, painted a line across the roof, and claimed one side was in California and the other side was in Nevada, thus being legal for slot machines and gambling. This became a turnaround point when patrolling.

The building was made chiefly with four by eight plywood sheets which meant that two-by-fours ran along about four feet above floor level, with the sheets nailed to them. The dining room and kitchen were in California, with a thin wall of plywood separating the two halves.

A rat decided to make this his abode, to the annoyance of the owner who placed a pistol handy. When the rat happened to scurry along the two by four the owner grabbed his pistol and took a shot at the pest. However, the bullet passed through the plywood and hit the cook. Now the question arose as to which state had jurisdiction. From what I heard, Walt happened along and said that since Las Vegas was only a short distance away, why not let Nevada handle it? And so it was.

Walt may have been credited occasionally for some incidents he had not handled, but that is the price for being so well known and highly visible.

His career was unique, by any standards. He came on the Patrol while it was still young, he was sent to the desert which nobody else wanted, and he was on his own. He was responsible for the biggest area anyone could have, one which had seen two men killed only a dozen years before in a war of sheepmen versus cattlemen which was slow in healing, and his available working tools were at a minimum.

During his twenty-eight years on the Patrol it grew from a few hundred officers to a few thousand. The radio came into use, along with better cars, better equipment, better communications, and less severe working conditions. He helped pioneer the use of aircraft in traffic patrol, and during all this he helped to train several dozen new officers.

Yes, the "Iron Man" and the California Highway Patrol were meant for each other.

The flood of February 26, 1969

The Mojave River floods again. Water everywhere, nearly a half mile wide here, upriver from Helendale.

I radioed for GAFB to send this chopper to rescue the Harold Smith family, stranded at their house.

Shown at front is Bill Bender, a nearby neighbor and Jackie Smith, who is smiling happily to be safe on higher ground.

The Old Greenspot Café as it looked when the incident with "Doc" started. His car was parked about where the small coupe is shown. The CHP unit was parked in the pump aisle.

CHAPTER TWO
GUNS, DRUGS, AND FAREWELL – PART ONE

Rarely do officers talk about any shooting incident in which they were involved. It is over and done with, best forgotten but never forgotten.

Half a century has gone by as I write this, and for many years all the others have passed on since that night in late December when we found ourselves in a shootout we did not want, and with a man who had been and still was a friend of ours. In my mind I can see every face as though I had been with all four of those men only yesterday.

When it was over we bore no ill will toward Doc but felt a little sad that we would have to put him in jail on serious charges. I have read the Civil War ended the same way, with many of the combatants feeling relief and no resentment.

It had been rather uneventful during my evening shift, giving not the slightest hint that violence would be coming my way. Chief deputy Zeke Eblen had become bored and left the sheriff's office to Carl McNew who soon went home.

After working until past one a.m., I went to the bakery shop next door to the old sheriff's office on 7th st. to visit with Tony Zanetti, owner, and another night owl like the rest of us, to enjoy one of his fresh hot donuts.

Shortly we were saying "See you later" and I departed for home. We would see each other sooner than we thought.

Within minutes I was home and undressing when the phone started ringing. It was Tony calling. "Buzz," he said, "Doc Newman his here at the Greenspot Restaurant and he is acting funny. Can you come right away? I think we better take him home!"

I quickly slipped back into my uniform and drove to the gas station across the street where, through the big windows of the café I could see who was inside and where.

Only a few customers were inside, plus the cashier, a waitress, and my two friends who were seated near the front.

Everything seemed normal so I entered as though this was the end of my shift, then sat next to them to visit. Doc's conversation was almost nonsensical, and he appeared to be on a real "High."

We had suspected for some time that he was taking dope and might become hooked. Many doctors during those war years were terribly overworked, especially if they took night calls, and some took cocaine in order to keep going, but in the end, they paid a price.

Tony was begging Doc to let us take him home, to no avail, and Doc rambled on. Unexpectedly, he called to the waitress and ordered a graveyard stew. I sensed the words might be indicative of an unpleasant plan he had in mind.

With the stew finished, he finally agreed to let us take him home. Tony would drive the doctor's car and Doc would sit beside him, while I followed in the patrol car.

Everything seemed normal as I walked toward the CHP unit when something made me look back to see Tony running toward me, shouting, with fear in his voice.

"Buzz," he yelled, "He's got a gun! He's got a gun!" At that moment the green Chrysler shot away for the curb and sped off down the street.

Tony and I ran for the patrol car, jumped in, and took off in pursuit, but Doc had turned at the next corner and was gone.

I put out a radio call for assistance while we were cruising the area in search of our erstwhile friend who now had to be considered armed and dangerous.

During this search Tony was explaining what happened. He was barely seated when Doc reached under the seat, pulled out a pistol, shoved the barrel into Tony's ribs, and told him to get the Hell out,--and Tony GOT!

Finally deputy Eblen arrived and was apprised of the situation. He said he had passed the car south of town but hurried on, in response to my call. Probably he was lucky to keep going; to stop could have been fatal.

Deputy Carl McNew joined us, a man with a reputation as an old-style western lawman, and we would need him.

We all jumped into the sheriff's car, including Tony, who was unarmed and wearing his white baker's outfit, which I considered risky if there was to be any shooting.

South of town on #66 we found the Chrysler, stopped in the middle of an empty highway, facing toward Victorville, with Doc seated inside, still trying to start the motor, though by this time the battery was dead.

Our best move was to drive past for a distance, turn back, and stop fifty feet away with our headlights shining on the rear of the green sedan.

He chose to remain seated, giving us time to deploy and survey the scene. Tire marks showed he had been westbound on Yates Road at high speed, failed to see the road ended at #66 and slammed through the dirt berm at the west edge, ripping off the gas tank. He was able to back up as far as the pavement before the carburetor used up its gas. Literally, he ran out of gas and luck at the same time.

Zeke called out twice, telling Doc to come out with his hands up, receiving no response. Everything was quiet. I think we all sensed that trouble was about to start.

Suddenly the silence was broken when Doc leaped from his car and ran toward the police unit. Stopping suddenly, pistol upraised, he yelled, "All right, you sons of bitches, come and get it." He may have thought we were only two, not realizing we now were four.

With that he opened fire, shooting as fast as he could, aiming toward the shining headlights. Two bullets hit our car, one passed between Tony and Zeke, and we didn't know where the other three passed by.

It was strange the Doc chose to use almost the same words Wyatt Earp is said to have used at the start of the famous shootout at the OK Corral in Arizona some sixty years earlier.

We had no choice but to return fire, doing no real damage, but our extra guns may have thrown him off balance.

With his pistol emptied, Doc turned back to enter the car. When he stopped shooting, we stopped, but now that he was back inside we faced a greater risk; we had to rush him before he could grab another gun or reload. It was a risk we had to take, and without hesitation we three ran to the side of the sedan, ready to shoot, if necessary.

Thank heaven, Doc had quit and was being rather meek, an unusual attitude for him, indeed. We handcuffed him, searched his clothing, and examined him for possible wounds. We found no injury other than a heel had been shot off one shoe, causing a slight bruise, and a bullet hole was in a suitcoat pocket. Fortunately, a bottle of cocaine in the other pocket was unharmed. None of us had been hit.

After daylight we returned to study the scene. To my shock, I found McNew had not followed correct procedure and had gone too far to the north, putting us in our own crossfire. It was pure luck we weren't hit with 'friendly fire' from the other.

Victorville, circa 1947. Looking NE down 7th
Street, Just SW of "C" St.
The old sheriff's office is to the left of the left tree.
Looks like my old 1937 Ford "Woody" at front left.
Carl King's Signal Oil sign at right and below is
Bud Hetzler's Shell station.
Signs near 7th Street "Hotel Stewart" on left.
Drugs – Sodas on right is Doc Bowers. The top of
the sign for the Green Spot Motel has Air
Conditioned on it.

CHAPTER TWO – Con't.
GUNS, DRUGS, AND FAREWELL—PART TWO

I have never read of nor heard of anyone describing how it feels to be in a gunfight, especially one in which the principals all were on a first-name basis. During the action every thought revolves around an overwhelming feeling that we must put our antagonist down before he (or they) can shoot any of us. Nothing else matters, and time cannot be measured. The human brain is incapable of measuring elapsed time, especially when under stress, which is the reason people when testifying under oath in court have a terrible time trying to give an accurate estimate of elapsed time occurring during a stressful experience.

We were certain that Doc would come out of his car shooting, and fervently hoping he wouldn't. Thus, at the sound of his first pistol shot it seemed to me I couldn't react immediately, though actually I did. I was shooting a Winchester 30-30 carbine with which only two months before I had brought down a running deer with one shot at three times this distance, so each time I pulled the trigger I could not understand why I was missing. Carl McNew, a fine shot, also was firing his rifle, and he wasn't doing any better.

I realized later that we all were firing too fast, with Doc pulling the trigger as fast as he could, which means he easily could fire his six rounds in about two seconds or so. Under stress, time had lost its meaning, and we weren't doing the kind of shooting we had been trained to do. Our concern had been for each other. Had we been more deliberate I am sure Doc would have been brought down.

As it turned our, his right heel was bruised when the heel of his shoe was shot off, and a bullet had torn through the left pocked of his suit coat. His bottle of cocaine was in the right pocket, fortunately not harmed.

What happened to Doc? He was tried, convicted, and drew a rather light sentence of one year in the county jail. He lost his time off for good behavior because he was found with dope in his possession while at a prison work camp near Etiwanda where it was believed that some woman who had paid him a visit had slipped him the stuff.

Not long after his release he started for Victorville in an old car which also contained, according to investigators, a half-full gallon bottle of wine. This was almost exactly a year and a half since the trouble and, again, was late at night.

About a mile north of Devore, on the old two-lane road, and driving without lights, he drifted into the opposing lane where he crashed headlong into a southbound sedan, dying almost instantly. He was forty at the time.

We knew Doc had several guns hidden in various places around the desert, and it was felt he had a few grudges he might choose to settle with the help of one or two of those weapons. He had lost his license, his livelihood, everything.

I still have a letter of apology he wrote from jail in August, 1945. Accompanying this is a copy of that letter. After you read it, would you feel he could be dependable?

In my mind's eye I can still see each of us, each face, and Doc's, too. I am glad we did not hurt him, nor he, us. If he were to walk into my house today, he would be greeted as an old friend, but I know I always would be wary.

CHAPTER TWO – Con't
DOC: A VERY COMPLEX MAN – Part Three

There were many sides to Doc, so much so that none of his friends really knew him.

He was young, good-looking, brilliant, yet there was a hidden, dark side in his brain which for the most part was kept under control. However, he loved to play practical jokes whenever he could, but usually they were weird, macabre, often heartless.

For the three years I knew him it was evident from early on that this was a dangerous man, one possessed by changing moods which ranged from extreme egotism to unexplainable periods of altering moods, similar to manic-depressive condition.

An example of this was the way he played the piano. The sounds were not musical; on the contrary, it was like listening to something from a Satanic cult, all done in a minor key and clashing chords. Not once did I ever hear that man play a piece of recognizable music. Everything was improvised, as though by Satan's hand, in a fashion which would make the Funeral March sound like a gay Irish jig.

Even when treating his patients he sometimes did the unexpected and we officers were fair game in his book.

Taking a spill on a motorcycle is a common risk we faced. If we saw the bike was going down, we could climb onto the top side, grab the crash bar and hold on until the machine came to a stop. If we were lucky the damage to us might be only some "gravel rash," meaning a lot of raw, scraped skin.

One day CHP officer Bob G. went down, losing some hide here and there in places Bob could not reach, so we took him to Doc's office.

Now, gravel rash hurts like the dickens and should be treated with non-burning antiseptic, but Doc swabbed Bob from one end to the other with the hottest, most fiery, worst burning variety available. The suffering officer could only clench his teeth and groan.

Then Doc injected Bob with something he claimed was and anti-tetanus shot and told Bob what to do and not do for the next eight hours, including going home right now.

About one half hour later Doc received a frantic call, "Doc, this is Bob. I am afraid I have been hurt pretty bad internally!"

"Why is that?" Doc asked innocently, "What makes you think so?"

"My God," said Bob, "I just urinated a mess of blood!" Bob didn't get a reply, just loud laughter over the phone, which told Bob he had fallen victim to another of Doc's practical jokes. The injection was intended to dye the urine red. Bob later said the sight of it scared the heck out of him.

Here is Doc's letter, just as he wrote it in 1945 from his jail cell. After you have read it, you be the judge; could I trust him in the future, or - - - should I not?

Dear "Buzz" & "Tony:"-
I hardly know whether you would like my writing to you; yet I feel strongly disposed so far to presume on the old relation which existed between us as to express my earnest hope that you will not attach too much importance to my mouthings of December last--wherein I was not

mentally conscious of either my action or words. I am writing nothing but what you know quite well already; still a momentary feeling of disappointment may sometimes tempt a man to do himself a great injustice, and to think that his efforts toward friendship in the past, have been attended by no proportionate fruit.

Fellows, I hold in my own mind only a cloud of remorse at my past actions, none of which, may I assure you again, were motivated by any type of premeditation on my part.

Being in jail has taught me a great many things—not taught directly from these "cellmates" of mine--but from my observation of them, their crimes, their conversations. Yes, my "cellmates", vulgar of manner, underfed, underdressed, and underbred, heartless, Godless, Hell's delight; rude by day and lewd my night. Dirty-robed and pauper clad. Raving, ranting, rotten, money mad, a squirming herd of human flesh; crazed with avarice, lust and rum!

From these I am learning, learning silence from the talkative, toleration from the intolerant, honesty from the dishonest, temperance from the intemperant, patience from the restless, kindness from the unkind. Yes, "Buzz" and "Tony," I am learning.

Here, more than anywhere else in the world, the daily panorama of human existence—the unending procession of governmental extortions and chicanery, of commercial brigandages and throat-slittings, of theological ribaldries, or legal swindles and harlotries—is so inordinately extravagant, so perfectly brought up to the highest conceivable amperage. It is the circumstantial details, the embellishing touches of probability, the general air of scrupulous—yes, almost of pedantic -veracity –found here, which profounds me continuously. Yes, gentlemen, I am learning.

It is through no one's fault but my own, that I am forced (practically) to associate with such.

Here I am, a man supposed to be possessed of splendid talents, which I often abused; and of a sound judgment, the admonitions of which I often neglected; a man who, finally for a short space of time, succeeded only in an inferior department of my art, but who, in that department, succeeded preeminently.

Yes, Gentlemen, I am still, and have learned a great deal these past 8 months. May I again apologize for what I did.

Sincerely,

"Doc"

Winters in the thirties and forties were always severe. This was my old Model T Ford at Big Bear in the early thirties, but at times the snow was as deep in parts of the desert. Also, the old Model T Ford was used in the 1920's and 1930's to bring many folks across the Mojave Desert. It was the auto of choice and necessity for those with little money.

CHAPTER THREE
VICTORVILLE AS IT WAS

When I was first assigned to Victorville in the late summer of 1941 as a state traffic officer of the California Highway Patrol I was pleased to find here an amazingly easygoing attitude, one in which everyone got along quite well together.

There were small communities from Helendale to Lucerne Valley, cattle ranches, dude ranches, and assorted ranches scattered throughout the valley, with a total population of about four thousand souls, and all, regardless of origin, could go about as they pleased. Perhaps a common denominator helped bind them together, the desert.

Our desert was harsher in those days. Summer days were hotter and many winter days were terribly cold. Very few homes had "swamp coolers", and winter heating was done with wood fires or oil-burning stoves. Ponds froze over and at time could support ice skating. Night temperatures frequently dipped into zero figures and had a long previous history of doing so in early days.

The river was a seventy mile long forest of trees, undergrowth, wild berries, wild celery, countless birds, fox, raccoon, possum, and even an occasional deer or bear. It still retained the wild flavor of the nineteenth century when the first trappers came through.

Life doesn't say that everything shall be equal, but the desert in the early 1940's had a way of closing the gap. Everyone mingled during the day, but by evening most people had gone home, while others headed for the bars or some other recreation. There was no television, so such things as summer niteball games were big entertainment. We ballplayers enjoyed playing with and against all the guys. They, and the fans, all looked alike to us. If anything can be said about segregation at that time, it should be stated that this largely appeared to be a matter of personal choice, on the order of the expression that "Birds of a feather flock together." Those were great days in Victorville.

Long before the flood of 1938 the Southwest Cement Company had built a row of concrete houses which resembled the old railroad type of section house. These were provided to those of their employees of any race who wanted low-rent housing. The big flood filled these buildings with trash and water to a depth of three to four feet. After that, the company moved their employees elsewhere and left the old houses to stand for a number of years, virtually unused.

Pioneers started the original settlement close to the Mojave River, obviously to make use of its water. At that time it had no name. Like Topsy, it was "just growing."

Inevitably the little settlement became the older part of town and, as happens to older areas everywhere, it was left to the poorer people when the more fortunate moved away. It was never referred to as a "barrio" until fairly recently. In fact, the word had not come into usage. Even so, its early meaning simply meant an open area or neighborhood. Only when it was linked with the word, "Bajo" did it mean a slum.

In time Victorville was subdivided. No one could imagine the town would grow; it was supposed to be a sleepy desert town, a supply center for cattlemen, miners, and travelers.

Therefore, the street which eventually would be known as part of Route 66 was named "D" St. and the road adjacent to the river was named "E" St. In effect, this was the dividing factor for the community, not the presence of railroad tracks which merely served as a line of demarcation between two different life styles.

Apparently the subdividers wanted to forestall a similar change taking place in the newer part of town and their real estate contracts incorporated certain restrictions.

Nonetheless, in time this difference invaded the once newer parts of town, causing many older residents to move again, further away. This sort of thing is still going on. By 1994 the character and appearance of the area around 7th and D. Sts. had changed so drastically that a movement was started in an attempt to "revitalize" it. This will be interesting to watch.

Again, it is a fact that people tend to feel more comfortable among others of similar tastes and background. Does anyone seriously think the Kennedys and Clintons would willingly choose to live "Across the tracks" anywhere? Hardly! But they and their kind believe everyone else should.

During the war years the area continued to grow, yet Victorville held on to its character as a desert town where people could come for the kind of fun they wanted, whatever that might be. It wasn't "wide open," but came pretty close.

Mention has been made of a house of prostitution on "E" street, but that needs clarification.

For a number of years an old wooden two-story building was in steady use as a rooming house, bar, and as and Elk's Lodge. Many thought this was just a title bestowed upon it by the operator, Fred Curry, but he actually was able to charter it as a bonafide Elks Lodge.

Fred was a very personable black businessman who knew how to make a buck. By getting a BPOE charter he could get a liquor license and the law would tolerate a little gambling. After all, the bigger Elks Lodge in town had a pretty heavy poker game going much of the time, so why couldn't he allow an occasional crap game?

Thus he obtained a tacit agreement that gambling would be tolerated so long as it didn't get out of hand, nor cause violence or complaints.

All was quiet for a time, but greed stepped in and the gambling became heavy. At these times a guard would be posted outside to watch for lawmen who might appear to make arrests.

Finally some wives complained that their husbands were losing the family money in the dice games, so one night the deputies were tipped off that a big game was in progress.

Two deputies sneaked up on the watchman and grabbed him before he could make a sound. Then the sheriff's captain, Zeke Eblen, quietly slipped inside the building where he found seven men so intent on the rolling dice that none noticed him approaching.

They were on their hands and knees around a blanket on the floor, a small pile of money in the middle. Zeke was a big man, not one to tangle with, and when the put his foot squarely on those paper bills and coins the gamblers finally realized the law had arrived. Of course everyone knew him and he knew them, so when one looked up at Zeke he said, "Oh, Oh! That man is here!"

Some things have to be tolerated within limits. It was felt that if the clamps were put on Fred's place it wouldn't stop his customers from gambling in a potentially dangerous and unknown location elsewhere. It was a simple case of always knowing what was going on.

Prostitution during the war years and for a while after was present almost everywhere in San Bernardino County. Women would rent rooms in hotels, motels, and fleabag rooming houses where they could ply their trade. A couple of dude ranches toward Lucerne were strongly suspected of being engaged. They always had plenty of young women around.

Even Highway 66 was being used by female hitchhikers who were willing to go in either direction. Some were seen so often they acquired nicknames such as "Highway Hannah" or perhaps more specific titles. Their favorite targets were truck drivers. On occasion these women would be seen as far a Needles or Las Vegas, trying to thumb a ride back to Victorville or Barstow.

From time to time Fred's place might become a temporary abode for one or more prosties, and they, like the others, would circulate in town, looking for customers.

During the forties and early fifties Victorville was still a rather rough and ready little town, living on the memories of its cow town past. Even a few hitching posts remained. There were frequent bar fights, usually over the honor of some woman who had lost it long before, there were a few shootings, a train wreck or two, vehicle accidents beyond belief, even though gas was rationed, and we had only three or four full time police to handle everything. Consequently all available officers pitched in to help each other out, regardless of who might have primary jurisdiction. Also, to have the full cooperation of the citizens, a certain amount of tolerance was given to minor—and perhaps some not so minor—infractions.

This attitude paid off because everybody, regardless of race, lived in remarkable harmony with one another. The disturbances mentioned above were almost always within their own race and not racial.

To illustrate: A call was received that a woman was being killed at the "E" Street Elks Hall. Deputies immediately rushed over. Upon arriving, they found some black men holding another black man, while on the ground was a black woman, bleeding profusely from severe cuts across her back. Questioning witnesses brought out the details. The man had been chasing the woman around and around the house, with the woman screaming and the man slashing at her with a straight-edge razor. Just in time to save her life, the other fellows caught the man who then submitted quietly.

When asked by the deputies for his reason to cut her so badly, his response was, "I didn't mean to hurt her; I was just a-hittin' at her!" Apparently to him the razor was a small matter.

At no time was racism a factor in those disturbances, nor were they planned. Everyone got along, everyone worked who wanted to work, and lifelong friendships were established in the schools. Later, when some of these young men were killed in the war, there was pain and sorrow shared by all who knew them. No community could possible be more tightly knit.

Here I am sitting in the back room of the old sheriff's office, waiting for my partner to finish writing an accident report. Note the holes in the worn out linoleum. That old building received hard use.

CHAPTER FOUR
MY FIRST CLOSE CALL

Many police officers have lost their lives because they were too trusting. At some point early in their careers it is important for them to learn that all crooks are con artists; male, female, and even kids. Sadly, the very nature of the work makes it necessary to be distrustful, to be cynical, and to reserve judgment. Further, I hadn't been on the job very long when I learned never to turn my back on strangers.

We received a phone call at the sheriff's office in which the caller said a man had been seen trying to break into some parked cars and was now in the corner drug store. Deputy Zeke Eblen was busy at the moment and asked me to go get the man and bring him to the office. I walked the block to the drug store, saw the man a described, about thirty-five, fairly tall, slim, clean shaven, wearing a felt hat and a nice coat. In other words, just and ordinary sort of guy. He acted quite unconcerned when I asked him to follow me to the sheriff's office. I was completely thrown off guard by his attitude and appearance. It looked like the report was in error.

We walked side by side for half a block to the first alley where he fell behind me a couple of steps when suddenly I heard the sound of a fairly heavy metal hitting the pavement with a clatter and sliding noise. I looked to my right and saw a dark pistol still sliding away from us and I realized the subject had been the one to throw it.

By this time the man was running past me at full speed, but I had to recover the gun before taking up the chase. He quickly had a good head start and was running diagonally across Seventh

Street toward the Green Spot Restaurant where a Greyhound bus was unloading twenty or more passengers. He headed straight for the group, which obligingly parted to let him through, but immediately closed ranks, forcing me to go around them.

Now the stranger had crossed C Street and entered a dark alley next to the theater. With my luck, I expected people to come pouring out of the theatre, too.

It was time to get some help. The old sheriff's office was only two hundred feet away, and hopefully the deputy would be through shaving, so I drew my pistol and fired a round into the air and toward the open desert. Maybe, with a little more luck, our subject might think I was going to shoot him and would stop. Instead, still running he shed that coat and took off in overdrive. He shouldn't have been a crook, should have been trying out for the Olympics. The last I saw of him was his shirttails flapping as he cleared a six foot high backyard fence and disappeared between neighboring houses, making good his escape. I grabbed up his overcoat, the deputy arrived, and we spent the evening searching the area with no success.

We found no identification in or on the coat but it fit me beautifully and served as a constant reminder of the need to be always on my guard. We figured he had the gun handy in one of the pockets, unloaded. Had it been loaded, I might have caught a bullet in the back. Now I realized what Inspector White meant when he greeted us rookies at the CHP academy with these words, "Fellows, this is a business of blood and guts, and for God's sake, don't let it be yours!"

Still, three classmates would be killed in the first year.

It pays to heed the advice of the experienced!

Buzz with daughter Janet, age six weeks. An advantage of being a resident officer, being able to come home for lunch and a little time with the baby. Note the round shoulder patch.

Buzz Banks watching the passing cars on Old Highway 66. Traffic was quite light during the war years due to gasoline rationing. Patrolling still was done on the Harley Davidson motorcycle.

CHAPTER FIVE
ONE WAY TO GET THE OTHER'S ATTENTION

There are occasions when people we stop for a traffic violation seem to feel an obligation to be on their worst behavior, especially when liquor gets into their brains. Many drunks have been hauled off to jail when, if they had behaved, they might have been given a break. We can only help those who show a willingness to follow our suggestions, provided they still have reasonable control of their faculties. The charge of DWI does NOT require a falling down state of inebriation.

One evening my partner and I noticed a vehicle speeding south bound toward Cajon Summit. We turned around and started in pursuit, eventually getting it stopped on the other side of the hilltop, but when he finally pulled over, the driver did so on the wrong side of the road, near the edge of a dropoff.

We could smell the odor of alcohol coming from the interior, the occupants looked a bit bleary-eyed and had obvious signs that drinking must have been going on. Four men were seated inside, wearing business suits (Which, in the old days on U.S. #66 and #91 between Las Vegas and Los Angeles occasionally indicated they might be gangsters. More crooks and gangsters of assorted varieties traveled this route than any other in the U. S.). Therefore, a group of males in such attire was dealt with cautiously.

Gangsters of the Mafia type usually were cooperative because they did not want to be delayed, but these men were uncooperative and a bit "smart-ass" with their answers. However, it was alcohol talking, and I could see the driver was in no shape to drive. Unfortunately, the DWI rules of those days were too lenient to support the charge. All four were equally under the influence and could not be trusted to take the wheel. My intention was to try to figure out a way to give them a break, but they proved to be very exasperating.

When I asked which of them owned a fifth of whisky lying on the seat, they claimed they didn't know how it got there. I asked each one in turn and got the same negative response, so I reached in and took the bottle. Then I asked again, receiving a chorus of denial. "Well," I said, "since it is not yours, I guess that makes it mine. Right?" They had to agree, but I could see they thought I wanted it for myself, and they became still more arrogant.

The bottle was half full, the other half having provided a nip for them every now and then along the way. I had a purpose in mind so I stepped to the edge of the dropoff, threw the bottle up and away, drew my revolver and shot the falling bottle into a shower of liquor and broken glass.

From that moment I had their fullest cooperation. It was Yes, sir, officer and No, sir, officer and we will do exactly as you say, officer.

I then told the driver I would let him off with only a ticket for speeding if he would do exactly what I ordered. He was to proceed just ahead of me, staying in the right lane and not going fast, until we came to a café two miles ahead. There he was to go in, stay for one hour while drinking lots of coffee, and they were to behave, which is exactly what they did. I had also added that we would be watching.

Sometimes cooperation can only be achieved through a strong bit of applied psychology.

44

1947. Interior of the old Victorville sheriff's office, CHP officers Buzz Banks and Bob Garrison, writing his report.
The "Lost" license plate hanging on the wall is either late 1947 or for 1948. Some of the forms we used are on the shelves above.

Circa 1946. Buzz standing at rear of the old
sheriff's office. The small restroom is shown,
tacked onto the building. At the right edge of it is
the small window used by the prisoner to make his
escape.

CHAPTER SIX
IF ONLY THAT OLD SHERIFF'S OFFICE COULD TALK

Few old buildings achieve a personality in their lifetime, but the old Victorville Sheriff's office substation lived a unique life of its own. If only it could talk of the things it had seen during its more than a half century existence, emerging from a local farm building to house the local sheriff's office, courthouse, and many more public services.

Small towns always have unusual people, and those who worked out of that little shack were no different, but each had his or her own way of dealing with the job. Likewise, the "customers" usually behaved in strange ways, especially those who were under arrest and being booked.

Equally interesting were the many visitors who dropped in throughout the day and evening, some on business, others just to rest a bit and talk. These were local folks who had a business, or a ranch, or who worked for these employers. Nowhere could law enforcement enjoy better public relations than lawmen here enjoyed over all those years. Let's take a look at a few who used that old building.

Jack Brown was the deputy in charge in the very early forties. He had served a long and eventful career as a San Bernardino County deputy sheriff. He was one of the officers involved in the investigation of the last killing which took place in eastern San Bernardino County in what was known as the war between sheepmen and cattlemen. This trouble went on for several years when the cattlemen who had been the first to raise livestock in the desert resented the arrival of newcomers who brought sheep to this harsh land and started homesteading. There simply wasn't room for both.

Eventually the range wars were over, but the desert never was crime free, and in time Jack was sent to Victorville as commander of the substation.

There were three things Jack loved above all. First was his wife and little boy, also named Jack. The other two were evening games of pinochle and night-shooting jackrabbits, of which there was a plentiful supply.

During the war years of the early forties there always was an evening lull until the bars empty. During those hours three of four of us would cruise about, looking for rabbits. Most of us liked to use our service pistols for the practice, but Jack favored a twenty-two rifle. After an hour or two we would head back in. As we neared town, Jack would stick the rifle barrel out the passenger side window and fire off all the remaining rounds in the magazine. He never bothered to save a single bullet!

On other evenings we would get out the pinochle deck. Jack would always count on the five card kitty and would bid far beyond his holding cards, so he seldom won. But it was in all in fun, and no money was involved.

We put in long hours, nonetheless, and we always were on call. Those few evening hours were a respite before it was time to gather up some drunk drivers or quell a bar fight. About the time we crawled into bed the phone would ring and we would have to dress and respond to a traffic accident.

Doc Brown was another old time deputy who now was a special deputy working at the Greenspot bar as a sort of peace keeper in case the rowdies chose to misbehave.

With that kind of job he drank gallons of coffee each evening, but alas, it damaged his stomach, so he kept a huge jar of Alka-Seltzer in a cabinet over the sink. About twice each night he came in, opened the jar and fixed a glass of the stuff. We told him he was killing himself but he wouldn't slow down. Sure enough, he retired and was preparing to take a vacation trip when he keeled over and was gone. His retirement was all too short.

Deputy Carl McNew was probably one of the most unusual because he saw no reason to adapt to the changing rules of law enforcement. His law was the law of Wyatt Earp. He saw no reason to deal with it other than head on. For that purpose he wore a Colt .44 on his hip and two concealed weapons under his shirt. He wouldn't chase an escaping felon or prisoner when it was so much easier to shoot the subject, and he didn't miss.

He had no use for salt, and avoided it altogether. Once he observed a waitress shaking a few grains of salt into a ten gallon urn of coffee. From then on he would not drink restaurant coffee unless he saw it made in a glass coffee maker.

Salt is needed in the human system for normal health, but lack of it must have left him susceptible to blood poisoning because he lost the tips of two fingers from this cause as a result of infection from two minor cuts.

One evening the phone rang in that old office, bringing word that three of America's worst criminals were traveling northbound on Highway 66 and shortly would be approaching Victorville. This was in the mid-thirties and the wanted persons were as bad as any gang in America. The orders were to stop these gangsters before they reached Victorville.

In those days lawmen weren't bound by technicalities, so Carl and Stan Snedigar, the deputy in charge at that time, together with Red Black, a foreman at the cement plant who frequently served as a volunteer deputy, armed themselves with buckshot-loaded shotguns and other firearms, then drove south about a mile to the empty desert and set up an ambush.

These criminals were killers of the same ilk as Bonnie and Clyde, Dillinger, and "Pretty Boy" Floyd, all of whom were gunned down by the Feds or Texas Rangers in 1934, and the infamous "Ma" Barker and her son, Fred, who were blasted in an ostensible gunfight with the Feds in 1935. They all were killers with machine guns.

While waiting for the subjects, there apparently ensued a discussion as to how to take them into custody. Two of the deputies were for stopping the wanted men with red light and siren, but McNew said those men would shoot first and were more heavily armed. The deputies agreed they had no choice but to be the ones to shoot first.

Shortly the described car, a 1934 DeSoto, passed by whereupon the officers fell in behind, then pulled alongside and opened fire, killing all the occupants almost instantly. There were no formalities, no red lights, no sirens, no shouts to pull over, and there were no accusations that they took the law into their own hands. That's the way it was, just a mere sixty years ago.

Nowadays the police are ordered to effect a stop without shooting. But with killers such as these, turning on the red light would be tantamount to committing suicide. This leaves police two choices: One, turn in their badges immediately, or, two, do what has to be done and live a bit longer.

One of the tow truck drivers told me that the left side of the DeSoto had so many bullet holes there wasn't a place on it where he could place his hand without covering at least one hole.

At the other extreme we had a night watchman, deputized, who was afraid of his own shadow and ran back to the sheriff's office for help at the slightest excuse, but perhaps it was for the best. He never made an arrest on his own.

The judge's office was a tiny room, housing a huge desk and one chair. If someone should plead not guilty a trial would have to be held elsewhere, such as the Masonic Hall.

Judges throughout the desert were not legally trained, but were elected as "Justice of the Peace" by their neighbors through the normal election process. As a consequence all trials were speedy, simple, and straightforward,--unless the judge happened to be relatively uneducated, as happened in Barstow. He had been the high school janitor for years, so well liked by the kids that when he retired and ran for office he was elected by his former students.

On one occasion a friend of an accused drunk driver happened to make the mistake of standing beside his friend who was pleading guilty to the charge before the judge.

They stood side by side and both were sentenced to thirty days in jail. The mistake wasn't discovered until they had been hauled to the central jail, eighty miles away. When the booking officer asked him what he was charged with, he replied he sure didn't know.

Victorville judges made a few mistakes, too. One time an out-of-state speeder was brought forthwith before the court. The man plead guilty, whereupon the judge said the fine would be fifty dollars. At this the man said he didn't have that much, adding that he only had enough to get back to Illinois. "Well," said the judge, "How much do you have?" Thirty dollars," was the reply. "Tell you what I'll do. I'll split it with you." Declared the judge, thinking he was being Mr. Goodguy. When the man returned home we wrote a letter complaining the California police and the judge had a collusion going against non-residents. Well, it is certain the fellow needed a lot more than thirty bucks for that trip.

Originally the building had two rooms downstairs and one upstairs, with the latter providing a bedroom for the deputy in charge. Eventually a room was added at the back, slightly larger than the others, and an outhouse was a short walk to the rear.

Later a sewer system was introduced in Victorville and a tiny room with a toilet was tacked on to the back of the newer room. Civilization was on its way!

This small add-on was fully appreciated, especially by a young fellow arrested by a new CHP officer.

After being questioned for a few minutes the subject asked if he could go to the bathroom. "Sure," said the officer, "There it is, right through that back door."

With that our subject entered the restroom, closed the door, and never was seen again. He had crawled out through the small window at the back and beat a hasty retreat while the officer was filling out his arrest report.

Never again would that officer take his eyes off a prisoner until the guy was in physical custody. He took an awful kidding over that for weeks. One deputy left him a note in the typewriter, presumably left by the escapee, in which he thanks his benefactor for being so considerate. In return, he added, as a farewell gift the officer could keep the jacket he had left in the office.

At one time or another every lawman will make an embarrassing mistake he would like to forget, something which neither his peers nor the public is likely to do. It just goes with the territory; only the walls of the old sheriff's office are willing to forget.

CHAPTER SEVEN
DESERTS SEEM TO DEVELOP UNUSUAL PEOPLE

Deserts of the world have always been noted not only for their history but also for the unusual accomplishments achieved by those who lived or worked or fought in them.

Our own Mojave Desert is no exception. The first Spaniards who crossed it, the trappers who followed later, and were succeeded shortly by military men, all entered the history books.

After them came prospectors, miners, cattlemen, ranchers, lawmen, and once again, the military of every service branch. Even the Navy put in a base.

One of the most unusual and often exciting bases was the one at Muroc Dry Lake, later known as Edwards Air Force Base.

Located on the southwest corner of the desert, this base first was used to test vehicles on rails at jet speeds. Stopping these projectiles was a feat in itself.

Soon it was to become the testing and preparation area for the Bell X-1 which would be the first plane to fly faster than the speed of sound. This was an exciting period for those involved because all aircraft began to vibrate horribly at 700 mph and it appeared certain nothing with wings could stay together above 760 mph, the speed of sound at sea level.

Chuck Yeager, now a general, was the test pilot during this period. His book, "Yeager" tells it all, and I strongly recommend it to those who wish they could have led an exciting life. Chuck certainly had it, and the Mojave Desert played a very large part. I have had my share of exciting moments, but no one living in this twentieth century could come close to his, not even those who flew in outer space. He lived dangerously most of his life, much of it right here in our Mojave desert.

He liked to excel in everything he did, a fact I did not know when we joined forces one morning for a deer hunt in the San Bernardino mountains.

My group of hunters and the fellows he was with met by accident on a basin in the hills and decided to work as a team. Yeager had not been in this part before so we gave him a route leading up to a pass, while the rest of us took different paths upward. We would meet again at the pass before tackling the tallest ridge.

All of us were accustomed to moving slowly, stopping frequently to look and listen. All of us, that is, but Chuck.

We were about half way to the pass when up ahead we heard a number of shots being fired. Our first thoughts were that someone else was already there and we had driven a herd of deer right into their rifles, since several of the shots were so close together.

There was little we could do but make our way toward the meeting place when we saw Chuck burst out of the brush, coming downhill toward us. As he approached, he veered away from me and headed toward one of my partners.

I thought this odd until they came over to me and explained what had happened. It seemed Chuck had moved much faster than we, had come upon four bucks practicing the dueling which would take place in earnest when the annual breeding rut soon would begin. They were too engrossed to be wary and Chuck opened fire while the bucks scattered.

He used up all his ammunition, bringing down three but the fourth escaped. Now he was faced with a dilemma; would I, a police officer, report him to the game wardens for killing more than one?

First, he had to ask my friend how I would take it. He was assured that nothing would be done since we all had tags for them. Also, his group was welcome to all the animals. We didn't want the season to end so quickly. Then we moved on to his deer, helped to clean them, and tracked the fourth deer until we were satisfied that he had not been wounded. I guess that buck had lots of fun with his harem.

We also agreed that on any future hunts we would have to insist that Chuck must agree to stick by our side and not gallop off ahead.

Here I should tell a bit more about Pancho Barnes, the woman who owned a dude ranch she had started in 1933 near Muroc Dry Lake. She was a close friend of Yeager's.

I first met her when she made one of her occasional stops in Victorville to buy supplies for her ranch and restaurant. At her first few words I knew I was talking to another of the unusual people who made the desert their home.

With the passage of time I was to hear stories about her ranch, the girls, the parties, and a few rather fanciful tales which had to be dismissed until proven. Chiefly, however, Pancho was one who might be called a "salty" character with a heart of gold.

She, too, had led an exciting life as a flyer, rumrunner and gun smuggler, to name a few. It was obvious to me, even during a five minute talk on the sidewalk, that she was a very restless and energetic person. Her rough life had led her into a vocabulary which even a stevedore couldn't match.

Sometime in the mid-fifties she had to close and sell her ranch. I often wondered what had become of her until I read Yeager's book. People, such as she was, do not just sink into oblivion. Somewhere, somehow, they bob up again.

After giving up the ranch, Pancho virtually disappeared, while Chuck lost touch with her during his assignment in Europe. He tells that "toward the last she was living alone with her dog in a mobile home out on the Mojave, a desert rat to the end," adding "the saddest part about her passing a few years back was that it was nearly a week before her body was discovered inside her mobile home."

Chuck, I share your thoughts regarding her passing, but in truth I have known of many folks who found comfort in living alone in the desert. They live alone, and they die alone, but while they were alive the desert has provided them with a life of peace and quiet they may never have known before. For them, death is merely a continuation of this life.

May Pancho Barnes always rest in peace.

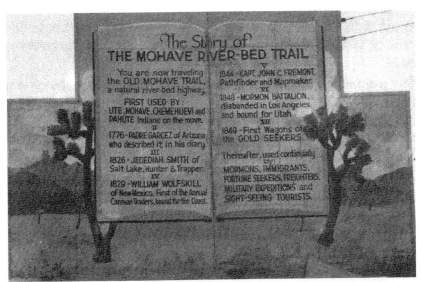

**One of the old roadside signs marking the historic Mojave Trail. There was time enough for passing motorists to read it.
The speed limit was only forty-five miles per hour.**

CHAPTER EIGHT
CROSSING THE MOJAVE DESERT HAD ITS PROBLEMS

Historians always recall the tough period in the nineteenth century when the covered wagon pioneers struggled to cross the Mojave Desert, but little is told of the days when the automobile came along and the few available roads were nothing more than wagon ruts left by wagon wheels.

Early travelers had to work their way out of trouble without the help of a passing police officer, for there were none. In fact, there was no real police force of any kind for any purpose. This brings up another point. Traffic officers are more than policemen, they are a helping hand to stranded motorists almost on a daily basis, especially in the desert. Radiators boil over, tires go flat, and gas tanks go dry, just to name a few.

Even here we run into tales of trickery and deceit perpetrated on our officers who have stopped to help, including shots being fired, or worse, and some that have been just plain unbelievably gross.

One incident involved a young woman standing beside a car with a flat tire, parked at the side of the road. She appeared helpless and distraught, so, being the gentleman he was, our officer stopped, took out the necessary tools from the patrol unit, and went to work switching her spare tire and wheel for the flat one.

As he finished and stood up, a neatly dressed man wearing a fine suit of clothes arose from behind a nearby bush where he had been hiding the entire time, said a quick thanks, got into the car and drove off, with both occupants smiling and waving at the disgusted officer.

Incidents such as these made me cautious. Whenever I saw any car at the side of the road, whether empty or occupied, I drove on by, looking it over carefully. Continuing past for some distance I would watch the mirror, then turn and go past the car once more before coming back a final time and stopping. One can't live to a ripe old age by being young, fearless, and foolish.

However, in the twenties and early thirties there were no friendly CHP units to help; motorists were strictly on their own, and the troubles were many. Frequently they spelled real trouble when the autos blundered into nothing more than wagon ruts. Cars and tires were very fragile, as were those pitiful wooden spoke wheels, all easily smashed.

Some tires were inflatable, others were merely solid strips of rubber which were cemented to a steel band that surrounded a wood wheel, much like a wagon wheel. Both types were weak, inefficient, and very troublesome.

Until the early twenties almost all the inflatable tires were what was know as the high pressure clincher type, meaning they had to carry much higher air pressure than do those of today, but the structural strength simply was not there, hence they didn't last long. Several spares were carried.

Special tools were needed to get them on or off because they had to be forced over the rim which then clinched the heavy bead so the tire couldn't slip around the wheel. A tube was used which first had to be properly placed and slightly inflated. A novice tire changer was likely to pinch or puncture it at this time, so tube repair materials were always carried along in his big bag of repair parts.

Las Vegas literally owes its existence to asphalt. Before paved highways came along no traveler cared to linger there. His destination was elsewhere, good roads or bad.

Oldtimers have told me some of the hardships encountered when driving from Las Vegas to Los Angeles.

First, the trip to Barstow took two to three days, provided nothing serious occurred. Camping out overnight was a must because the headlights were nearly worthless and it was too easy to have big trouble in the dark. Furthermore, camp had to be set up during daylight. Also, in the winter it could be bitter cold. The open touring cars of the day gave no protection, and heaters hadn't been invented yet.

Sometimes the kids huddled under a blanket, usually at the back seat, trying to stay warm. Unfortunately, on occasion one or more would die from carbon monoxide poisoning because gases were trapped during those times when the motor was running. Frequent tire failures were the norm, while any major breakdown could mean leaving the car. Repair shops along the way were scarce to none, and parts might not exist anywhere.

Along the way were countless washes which had to be crossed, many of them having been recently flooded, leaving vertical walls too high to traverse. In such cases a detour had to be found or a lot of shoveling was in order.

Added to the problems presented by nature, the tires were quite narrow and would sink deep into loose sand or mud, frequently sinking too deep for the car to move. About this time the air might turn blue when the delay turned into hard work for the occupants. These tires usually were called size 30x3 or 30x3- ½ , which meant the wheel diameter was about thirty inches and the tire diameter was approximately 3 inches. The actual tread width was less than three inches. Heavier cars had only slightly larger tire dimensions. All could sink deep into the sand. Today many offroad tires are very large and carry low air pressures so the vehicle can stay atop the sand.

Travel from present Victorville to San Bernardino could take a day, as could the remainder of the route to L.A., even though the latter roads were more frequently used.

I have a 1910 road map which states that along the San Bernardino – Los Angeles route were a number of narrow washes where there were two steel beams to serve as a bridge which might have to be re-adjusted to conform to the width of different axles since the last car over them may have had a wider or narrower axle. Apparently in those days nobody stole the beams.

Between the front and rear fenders on those old cars were steps called running boards. These were needed to get up into the vehicle which stood so high from the ground most folks couldn't step up that high, especially women wearing the ankle-length dresses of the period.

Any time a long or tough trip was planned a folding metal guard would be secured to the step, which acted like a gate to hold extra gas cans, tools and provisions. Those old autos were so loaded down they could be mistaken for a sort of rescue mission going out to help somebody else.

Yes, indeed, crossing the desert spelled ADVENTURE, and helpful traffic cops were far in the future.

The Mojave Desert and Highway 66 known as the "National Trails Highway." Photo shown is just north of the Highway 395 turnoff. How sweet it was to have an empty desert and lots of healthy Joshua Trees! This was in the nineteen forties. The squad car pictured is a 1949 Buick.

The famous old Victorville sheriff's office as it
appeared in 1947. It had been in use for many
years but shortly would start a new tho' neglected
life as a real estate office in Apple Valley, serving
chiefly as a curiosity attraction.

CHAPTER NINE
JUDGE ROY BEAN WOULD HAVE LOVED VICTORVILLE

Easterners passing through Victorville during the war years found a town still clinging to the old west tradition, including the sheriff's office which proclaimed its identity with a small sign over the porch of a ramshackle wooden building facing the main street. Except for the two huge cottonwood trees growing at the front, its appearance immediately reminded travelers of old pictures where the famous Judge Roy Bean held forth in a very similar shack in which he held "court" and handed out his "Law west of the Pecos."

Other similarities may have taken place, at least in the minds of some folks who had committed offenses, only to find themselves being tried by the justice of the peace in a very brief and informal trial, after which they might be hauled off to jail.

Space inside was limited to three small rooms downstairs and a bedroom upstairs used by the deputy in charge. None were large enough to hold a jury, and usually nobody bothered to ask for a jury trial. The judge held court in the little front room with a rolltop desk so huge it occupied a third of the space and stood so tall the judge was hidden behind it. This gentleman, a tall, thin, elderly grey-haired man was named, appropriately enough, J. P. Hoffman and he was just that, a Justice of the Peace. However, he maintained the manner and dignity one would expect from a member of the Supreme Court.

Here western justice was dispensed in a small desert town which was slowly emerging from its past.

Victorville was starting to feel growing pains and might have seen more rapid growth had not World War Two put the brakes on for a time, even though George Air Force Base started up, bringing in a large number of personnel.

Long after the old building was moved to Apple Valley, to be used there as a real estate office with a western motif, it was sorely missed. Everybody had dropped in almost daily, whether to conduct business or simply say hello.

Through the years of WWII it also was shared by the Highway Patrol, Red Cross, Military Police, Constable, welfare, marriage parlor, brand inspector, and other services of county government. By 1945 the linoleum was worn through to the wood floor underneath. If only that old shack could talk! So many unusual incidents took place over its decades as a public office. Many were unbelievably funny, others were sad, and often they were cases of helping people who felt they had nowhere else to turn.

One day in 1942 a motorcycle wheeled up in front and a man wearing a military uniform, hard helmet, and two pearl-handled pistols in holsters, leaped off the bike and strode through the front door to ask directions. This was General George S. Patton, leading the first troops to be trained in the Mojave Desert for the coming desert warfare in North Africa.

Within moments he was on his way, and about fifteen minutes later the main military convoy appeared.

I was shocked when I saw his convoy. Most of it was nothing more than ordinary flatbed one and a half ton olive drab trucks with side racks, carrying supplies and GI's. A number of the trucks also carried a wood two-by-four about ten feet long, projecting out over the cab. I had to ask, "What in the world are those things supposed to do?" "Well," I was told, "They represent antiaircraft guns and cannon. We don't have enough of the real thing!" The U.S. army was so poorly equipped at the time of Pearl Harbor its military had to train in part with simulated weapons.

Our local baker was so happy to see those soldiers he brought out pan after pan of fresh donuts which he held up as he walked alongside the trucks, telling the men to help themselves. They didn't hesitate to reach down for these unexpected treats and doubtless they always remembered his hospitality of Victorville and a man they did not know. The baker was Tony Zanetti.

In that old shack called a sheriff's office one could easily see how alcohol does different things to different people. Some were in a happy mood while being booked, others wanted to fight. Few ever admitted to being intoxicated. One drunk driver fancied himself on opera singer and sang Pagliacci all the while he was being booked. He still was singing opera as he was hauled off to jail.

Many good solid arrests were made by the officers simply by sitting on the front porch, watching the traffic and the people passing by.

On a warm summer day two deputies were seated in the shade of the porch when one noticed a young man walking past. The deputy suddenly said, "I'll bet that is the guy we have boon looking for on those pay phone knockovers!" He stepped over to the man, took him by the arm, and steered him to the porch.

Patting the guy's pockets, he said, "What have you got in your pockets, fella?" The man was white as a sheet. Without a word, he pulled from his pockets a large quantity of nickels, dimes and quarters. After all the coins were out, he admitted stealing them from pay phones.

It was good police work. The deputy had noticed the bulging pants and the sagging effect caused by the weight of all those coins. When things seem wrong, find out why.

During those early years of the forties we made our own working hours and to some it may have seemed like an easy life, but we put in long hours each day, working according to the shifting needs, and we always were on call, day or night. Thus, at quiet moments we might rest our bodies on the porch, but our eyes and brains were active. Somebody somewhere is always doing something wrong, and they always leave the scene. Literally, they came to us.

On another day my partner and I were cooling ourselves on the porch when I noticed a sedan passing by with a solo occupant, the driver. For no reason I can exactly explain I felt the car was stolen. I jumped to my feet and yelled, "Let's catch that guy. I'll bet he stole that Chevy,"

We ran out to the curb fired up our motorcycles, and quickly had him pulled over, much to his surprise. He had good reason to be surprised; he had just stolen it from a parking space around the corner. We had recovered the Chevy before the owner knew it was gone.

While we were booking the suspect the owner came dashing in to report his car had been stolen. He was amazed we already had it waiting for him.

Well, the day was still young; what else could we find?

About late 1942. The Barstow sub-station squad of the California Highway Patrol, celebrating its beginning. This photo was taken in front of the Barstow High School.

CHAPTER TEN
TO BATHE OR NOT TO BATHE

Much has been said about barrios and the alleged mistreatment of various minorities. In reality, every one of us who is or are citizens of the United States should see ourselves as the most fortunate people in the world today.

In our land those who do not try to move ahead or set goals for themselves should not blame others when they find themselves left behind. Further, segregation is NOT due to race or color, as some think, but comes about for other reasons, the primary ones being differences in lifestyle, health habits, language barriers, and education.

At the turn of the century most of Southern California was still cattle country, especially the huge Mojave Desert. As such, it was a rough environment to live in and to work in, yet that very toughness was the kind which tends to knit folks together when they share a common hardship.

When we moved to Victorville in 1941 we found it still was a small and friendly town which clung to its past, though WWII was about to bring an end to all but memories.

After having lived in many California locations I found to my surprise that here was a mixed racial group which was living in better harmony than I had seen anywhere.

It is true that the residents of "E" street were mostly of Mexican descent, along with a very few Afro-Americans, with most of the latter living in North Apple Valley and Bell Mountain. The famous "Murray's Dude Ranch" was known throughout the country as the only such ranch expressly catering to the black population. Mr. and Mrs. Murray were always welcome when they came to town, as were their many famous guests of the time.

During its early days most of Victorville was along "E" street, including its bars, hotels, stores, and the like.

Inevitably the new becomes old and people move on to new places much as they discard old clothes for new. Thus those who wanted better than the old original shacks would move to the newer section, leaving behind the poorer folks who could afford nothing better.

Few of those old shacks had running water and bathtubs, while many had only dirt floors. When I first walked into one of those homes I was shocked to see mattresses on the dirt floor which were beds for all, some occupied by a many as five small children. Screens were torn out, doors hung loose by one hinge, and an air of dampness permeated the interior as rising moisture from the river came up through the floor.

Tuberculosis was a common sickness among these families in those days.

Though most of the men worked at local jobs which paid the same wages to all, the lifestyles varied widely.

Major differences such as this will always tend to separate people, regardless of race or color. The old saying, "Birds of a feather flock together" is true for more than just birds, and when the day's work is done we tend to be like the birds, heading for our homes and the haven they provide, whether home is a mansion, a cottage, or a rented room.

It also became apparent that as time progressed and some of the children became better educated they chose to move away from "E" st. to live a better life. Nothing held them back. Others chose to stay and fix up their homes.

There was no law forbidding the sale of real property to minorities, written or otherwise, but real estate development contracts often had clauses included which forbade any buyer from reselling to any minority. Simply stated, no one wanted to be the first to do anything which might start a decline in neighborhood values, hence white areas tended to remain white until that no longer was possible and they moved away once again.

If I were to pick out one thing which caused the most problems for ethnics in Victorville it would be the scarcity of bathtubs in those "E" street houses. Yes, bathtubs!

As a police officer, there were some oddities I felt I deserved a few inquiries because of their apparent racial segregation. These seemed at odds with the general attitude of the townspeople toward minorities and I wanted to know why. Usually there is some underlying reason why people adopt rules or attitudes. I needed answers.

Only people with white skin were allowed in the privately owned Crystal Plunge in town. I asked Mrs. Chantry, the owner why this was. She told me that too many of the residents across the tracks tended to use the pool as a bathtub, so she had to refuse them admittance.

For the same reason a similar rule was imposed when the first high school plunge was built. Only white kids could use it the first four days of the week. Any and all could use it on Fridays because the pool would be drained and scrubbed on Saturday.

Likewise, the local theater had a rule requiring members of minorities to sit only in the seats to the left side of the aisle. I asked Mr. L.M. Perkins, the owner, why he had this rule. He responded that due to their lack of bathing, too many of the minority folks had strong B.O. which made it unpleasant for others who might sit next to them. I must admit, on occasion the air in the old theater could get a bit heavy, regardless of the seating location.

Those who rarely take a bath fail to understand why anyone should fuss about it, but where cleanliness can be forced upon others, it usually is. It is said that in the days of royalty in France, only their ruling class saw fit to bathe on Saturday night, whether it was needed or not.

To bring home the point, and this could very well describe early Victorville: We once lived in Ramona, a cattle town two blocks long on an all-dirt dusty street, no electricity, and a one-room telephone office. The telephone girls recognized every voice and in turn, we knew them. One long cranking was for the operator, while a system of shorts and longs reached those on your party line. The only trouble with this was that everyone loves gossip, so regardless of who was being called, all would listen in. On important calls the caller would have to beg the others to hang up as the signal was too weak to carry the voices of the principals.

Well, this was a part of early California, and so were the cowboys.

Cowboying was something of an itinerant occupation because, though the ranches were large, the need for ranch help varied almost daily, and those who liked the wandering life would ride from one ranch to the next on a trip of thirty miles or more each day. If we had some work, we hired them for a few days. They were always made welcome, however, and invited to stable their horses, feed them, and put their gear in the bunkhouse. Mom would tell them we would have hot water ready for their bath (hint) and dinner would be served a bit later.

After breakfast these men would saddle their horses, bid us goodbye, and be on their way. None were refused this hospitality at any of the ranches. Those who didn't care to at least "wash up" didn't eat at the table with the family; the food was taken to the bunkhouse or out on the porch.

There are few animals in this world that can rival the odor of a cowboy who has been on a weeklong cattledrive. He had little time for anything but work, eat, and catch a quick nap. The eight hour workday was unknown while thirty dollars a month and found was the rate of pay, and all the dust he could eat.

When a cowboy came to town, a room and a bath were usually his first priorities. Without a bath, he might be treated like a pariah. After his bath, usually at the barber shop, his next priority was a shave and maybe a haircut. Often the only bathtub in the hotel was "down at the end of the hall" and not always available. John Wayne had it easy.

How come John Wayne was always so clean in his movies? Could it be he learned to take a bath as a kid?

CHAPTER ELEVEN
WHEN CALIFORNIA WAS INVADED FROM THE MIDWEST

Few people today can remember the depression of the thirties, and even fewer saw the migration of Americans coming into California.

Though they came from many states, the bulk of them were from Oklahoma, hence they all were termed Okies. This story is not to disparage anyone from any state, rather I am trying to tell it as it was. In fact, many of us were as poor as were they, but it happened we were already living here.

The first and most famous influx occurred during and after the Midwest drouth which was nicknamed the "Dust Bowl" because the topsoil of the farms literally blew away, leaving sterile land which could not grow crops.

Farm owners lost their land through bank repossessions, workers had no jobs, so they packed up their few possessions and headed west.

Many jokes arose because they arrived penniless. At one point our state officials tried to turn them back at the California Border Inspection Station. These were sad days for folks who had lost everything. When a bedraggled old car approached, the "natives" might say, "Gee, here comes a rich Okie; he has TWO mattresses tied on top of that thing!"

Or they might pull into a tire shop, pull out a tire so torn to pieces it looked like a rag, and ask, "Do you have a good used casin' and toobe?" with just such drawn out words. The poor guy looked beat, tired, worn out, and penniless.

Many of them could go no further and would camp by a stream or wherever they could, then look for work locally. Those folks rarely begged, they just wanted work to earn the pennies their families needed for food.

Fortunately, food was very cheap. A dime could buy a gallon of milk, or a large loaf of bread, while fruit and vegetables rotted in the fields, free for the taking. There were no buyers. However, wages were as little as a dollar a day, with plenty of unemployed willing to work for anything. They were desperate to feed the family.

Bakersfield was the destination for many, and one joke asked, "What are the first three words an Okie baby learns to say? Answer, 'Mommy. Daddy. Bakersfield!!"

Some got as far as the Mojave Desert towns and stayed. Many became successful businessmen, bought acreage, and put signs up bearing their names at the driveway entrances, driveways which later became city streets which kept their names.

Hughes Road and Batson Place are two roads in Victorville named in such fashion, though these families came in about the time of the second migration of 1941 when the war industries coaxed them to California. A few more came after the war because jobs still were available. Some of these folks started prosperous businesses also. They seemed to see opportunities overlooked by locals.

Desert towns really benefited from these migrations, whereas the jokes were nothing more than humor at the time and the conditions which existed. John Steinbeck found the less fortunate families worthy of a great book about the lives of those who settled in Bakersfield and the San Joaquin Valley. He saw no humor in their plight.

Times were so tough some hitchhikers were said to be seen holding up both thumbs, willing to go in either direction.

However, there was a different kind of visitor, a wanderer of the railroads, who came from many states and drifted west in the wintertime where the climate was more to their liking. During the thirties and forties Victorville was a mecca for these itinerants, known as hobos. At times they became nuisances. They would accost people near the post office or stores and ask for money. Others liked to go from house to house, begging for food. This was an easy touch because many housewives had known what it was like to be without food. And the panhandlers knew there were many easy "marks" who simply could not bear to turn them away. Some of the bums professed to be willing to work for a meal, but the only calluses on their palms were from grabbing handholds on the railroad freight cars. They even marked the homes with symbols which told other hobos such things as which occupants would give food, or not, or had mean dogs, and so on. They had a hobo jungle at the Narrows, between the railroad tracks and the river, complete with a few cooking utensils, an old mattress or two, and discarded sofa cushions to rest upon. We had to warn the kids to avoid the place for their own safety, but kids are kids and many sneaked a peek or two.

In those years we had what was known as the vagrancy law which entitled us to arrest them if they were drunk or were bothering people. Most of the cash they bummed from folks went for cheap wine. After drinking it at the park they would pass out on a bench where they would be arrested.

One night I helped a deputy gather up such a drunk. We had a problem because he was too big to carry, and we could not awaken him. He was lying on a table, toes up. I rapped the soles of his shoes with my nightstick but he was too far gone to come out of his stupor. I banged once more, quite a bit harder. This had the desired effect and he was able to limp, with our help, to the patrol car.

Following a free breakfast next morning at county expense, he was brought to the old sheriff's office to await his moment before the judge. While sitting on a wooden bench he removed his shoes and vigorously rubbed the soles of his feet. I looked at him and felt I should say nothing. He saw me watching him and said, "Boy, I must have banged my feet on something last night, but I was too drunk to know what."

Soon he was called into what passed for a courtroom where the judge passed the usual sentence of those days, "Get out of town today and don't come back!"

There was little likelihood he could do anything that day but languish in a hobo jungle. As for me, I never again used the nightstick for any reason.

Tools of the Trade

C

Typical tools of the police officers in the early days, a "six-shooter' with belt, holster, handcuffs, and a pair of handcuff keys. There wasn't much else. No, this is not the famous Colt Bisley.

CHAPTER TWELVE
CARL MCNEW; VICTORVILLE'S QUIET PISTOLERO

From the time of Wyatt Earp the rules covering lawmen in their physical contacts with lawbreakers have been steadily tightening. Shooting at felons can be done only under limited situations, whereas only fifty years ago an escaping felon need not be pursued in a footrace if it was quicker and easier to shoot him. Before that it was considered the right thing to do. Only Superman could outrun a speeding bullet.

Deputy sheriff Carl McNew was born to a time warp. His attitude toward law enforcement was 1880 style, rather than the nineteen-thirties. However, there were a few times when this old-fashioned belief in self preservation undoubtedly saved his life. He was not given to mentally debating a problem in his own mind. To him the answer was a simple one,--act first and right now, though at times the only act he knew was to shoot.

In his way Carl was an anachronism who managed to do his job his way in a world which was changing under him. Had he not slowed down a bit as he grew older, he easily could have found himself on the wrong side of the law, however unintentional the cause might have been.

Outwardly, Carl McNew was quiet, mild-mannered, and unassuming, yet on his right hip he carried a beautiful Colt .44 Bisley revolver, while under a loosely fitting blue shirt were two more pistols, hidden from sight. He selected these shirts carefully. They had to have nine buttons down the front, plus two pockets, or he wouldn't buy them. Pants had to measure exactly eleven inches from crotch to waistband, and of course they had to fit. These were not idiosyncrasies but were necessary for quick access to the hidden guns. Nor could the pants bulge nor bag in a way which might interfere with a fast draw when he went for that Colt.

Oddly, he was a good but not great target shooter. However, just put a nail in a board, have Carl back off about fifteen feet, then watch him draw and shoot, punching that nail right through the board with a single shot.

There is no doubt about it, Carl was one of the deadliest lawmen I ever have known, not as a killer but as a shootist with nerves of steel who was ready to kill if he felt it was his only choice. Nothing ever excited him.

One night near the end of the nineteen-thirties he was told he would have to take a freshly arrested felon to the main jail in San Bernardino because the man was far too dangerous to be put in the local lockup. A man who happened to be present said he needed a ride down and asked if he could go along.

Nowadays this would have to be refused, but this was during the free and easy days when such things were oke.

The three piled into the front seat of the police car, Carl driving, the subject on the right and the passenger in the middle between them. Whoever shook down the prisoner didn't do a very good job, as it turned out.

Just below Blue Cut, in Cajon Pass, the prisoner slipped off the handcuffs, which some crooks have learned to do quite easily, pulled out his hidden pistol, pointed it at Carl while yelling at him to pull off the road and stop.

Carl obeyed the command, but the crook made the mistake of keeping his hand on Carl's pistol, thinking it was the only weapon the deputy had. He undoubtedly planned to yank it loose as soon as they stopped.

It began to look like the deputy and the passenger would never see the next sunrise, but that wasn't the way Carl saw it. He stopped the car with a jerk, throwing the others off balance, while at that moment he swung open his door, leaped out, drew a hidden pistol with his left hand and fired across the stomach of a thoroughly frightened passenger. His bullet was effective but not fatal, while the middle man probably was deciding that hitching a ride in a police car wasn't a very good idea.

McNew picked up the microphone and in a perfectly normal voice said, "Change my destination for the county jail to the county hospital." The lads in the radio room asked no questions. They simply turned to each other and said, "It looks like Carl has shot another one!"

There is a saying that old time gun slingers had one thing in common; they lacked fear. I believe Carl shared that feeling. Maybe he was just darn sure of himself. If he had missed the crook, or shot the passenger, their lives would not have been worth a plugged nickel –or not a plugged crook.

Everything about McNew would lead a stranger to misjudge the man. He was about six feet tall but looked shorter because he seldom straightened up, yet he carried no fat on his bones. The baggy shirt and slight shuffle, along with a chewed up matchstick always held in his mouth, added to his appearance of a simple country boy lawman who probably got his job through a relative on the Board of Supervisors.

Carl rarely had anything to say in public, but within the walls of the old sheriff's office he felt at ease and could tell many tales of the earlier days when the Indians still lived in or near Victorville and used their bows and arrows to shoot jackrabbits while riding bareback on a pony. He had many stories of the local Indians and certainly increased my knowledge of the Indian way of life here.

His eyes could be friendly or they could be cold. They were a steely blue which somehow seemed to scare the wrongdoers when he simply looked at them. The local tough guys didn't want to cross this man.

One such fellow made this mistake by trying his luck while being taken to the old jail on "E" St. for a minor violation.

Carl had left the man seated in the car while he went to the big steel door which always was locked on the outside with a huge padlock weighing two pounds or more. It took a huge key to lock or unlock it.

Opening this door meant turning his back on the prisoner who, in this case, decided to make a run for it, but his feet hit the ground rather noisily as he ran. Carl heard him running, turned, drew, and shot. Not wanting to kill the man, he simply fired at a leg, which stopped any further attempt to run, but the fellow suffered a damaged knee which caused a lifetime limp.

If this were to happen today, Carl would have to face charges, but that was then, not now, and it was a different world altogether.

San Bernardino was still a "cow county" in fact and in spirit. None of the deputies wore uniforms at work, favoring cowboy hats and western gambler style attire. They easily could hire on as movie extras in a western film without changing anything.

In this atmosphere it is easy to understand how a man like Carl, born to the nineteenth century in spirit, could conduct himself in that manner in the twentieth century. It is with both nostalgia and sadness that I know there will never again be the like of Carl McNew in this lifetime.

It has been a privilege to work with, and to have him as a friend.

CHAPTER THIRTEEN
HARD WORK AND HARD ROCKS

Guy Wadsworth was one of the hardest-working men I have ever met, hard as the rocks he worked with and almost as unforgiving toward those he disliked or distrusted.

His business, literally, was rocks and more rocks. He operated sand, gravel, and rock quarries in and around Victorville, doing his own tractoring, blading, loading, hauling, and delivering.

It wasn't an easy life for a man in his late forties, but "Waddie" was equal to it. Old faded overalls and a blue work shirt covered a six foot frame carrying muscle, sinew, and sweat.

Waddie never played, never went to the bars, never did much of anything but work. When business was slack he built rock houses and rock water towers, as solid and enduring as granite can be.

What makes a man live only to work? I often wondered. Every personality offers psychologists something different to study, but they haven't paid much attention to those who love little else than hard physical effort.

There was no chance to learn anything about Waddie's past except older deputies had said that during Prohibition days he had done some bootlegging around Guasti, west of San Bernardino, had been arrested a few times, and as a consequence did not like lawmen. Some folks believed he continued with that activity long after prohibition ended, but none of the deputies believed he was so engaged, though he may have maintained a somewhat private stock.
Furthermore, all bootleggers, large or small, had to seek other employment as legal liquor was cheaper

than the illegal stuff. They were put out of business.

For a long time Waddie's business was mostly done at some distance from Victorville, but after the war developers became very active and needed sand and gravel. More and more I would see his truck, usually without proper equipment, pass by. I knew rocks and gravel are tough on trucks, so I could only hope he would repair the broken items, but it didn't happen.

Finally I had no choice. He was stopped and given what the CHP called a mechanical notice, which is simply a notice to make the repairs and have the ticket copy certified by any officer, showing the violations had been corrected. No court appearance would be required except for failure to comply.

Waddie was visibly annoyed, signed the notice, and drove off with scarcely a word.

About a year or two later things were back at square one; his truck had been repaired but before long it had a sizable list of vehicular violations I could not ignore.

Again I chose to write a "mechanical" rather than a citation. This time he spoke up saying, "Banks, you've got it in for me!" To this I responded, "No way, Waddie. I know you have to make a living, so you won't have to go see the judge, but you've got to keep your trucks legal. Everybody sees them and knows I am supposed to do something about it, so that puts you and me in the same boat. All I am asking of you is to keep your equipment legal."

I must have said the right thing. From then on his truck could pass inspection at any time, and sometimes he would even wave at me.

Time went by, I would see Waddie at work with his tractor or driving by, and soon he had a third rock house completed, hear Helendale, complete with a two-story rock tower which supported a large metal water tank atop the structure.

Finally a near-miracle occurred; he took some time off to make a trip back east with his wife. Then a second miracle took place when in my mail was a package from them containing a nice little gift, one of those souvenir items with the name of an eastern town displayed. A man who did not like cops had sent me,--me, a cop, a token of friendship!

More time passed, and things seemed to return to normal when on a cool evening I received notice that a phone call had come in for me from Mrs. Wadsworth, asking me to call.

Puzzled, I immediately returned her call. All she could say was that Waddie wanted to talk to me and would I please come over right away.

Upon arriving at the rock house I found the yard lights on and Mrs. W. waiting in the doorway, Waddie behind her. After the greetings, she asked me to come in as they had something to tell me.

As a police officer, I had become accustomed to the unusual, but this message was not like Waddie at all.

Almost immediately upon my entering the living room and being seated, Waddie arose and went into the next room. Mrs. W. had a small white cardboard carton on her lap which she held as she started talking. First, she apologized for her husband leaving the room, saying he wanted her to do the talking, then went on to say that both of them were afraid Waddie was losing his mind and was fearful he might kill her.

She opened the box, disclosing a black nightgown. Holding it up for a better look, she said, "Waddie bought this for me to wear and told me that if he should start to attack me at night I am to run out into the darkness and hide so he can't see me. He doesn't really want to kill me, but is afraid he might. But if this should happen, we want you to know so you can tell the other policemen that he didn't mean to do it; --he just wasn't responsible."

As I listened to her I felt sad for both of them. It was obvious that a crisis of some kind was in the making. What made it worse was that she was such a tiny woman who, to my eyes, looked very fragile, yet willing to stay with her husband and accept whatever fate had in store for her.

Some might say Waddie was setting up a plan to provide him with an alibi for later murdering her, but I could feel a genuine sense of foreboding from both of them. I gave her my promise and my wishes for the best, then left, hoping their fears were unfounded.

Not very long after, I learned Waddie had died when his tractor rolled over and crushed him. I knew this was strange because that kind of tractor, a rubber-tired Fordson, was well known for its habit of rolling over when operated parallel along a sidehill, due to a high center of gravity, and I know he would know that. Investigation of the accident disclosed Waddie was doing just that when the tractor rolled over on him.

I believed then, and do now, that Guy Wadsworth was afraid of what he might do to his wife, and chose this way to end his life,- "accidentally," rather than risk causing harm to his loved one.

Cajon Pass, just north of Blue Cut (The San Andreas Earthquake Fault.)
Photo taken about 1914. This was long before it became U. S. #66. The road surface is not asphalt but a kind of oil scattered over the dirt. It was known as El Cajon Pass, Spanish for "The chest of drawers." Perhaps the long canyon between two mountains gave rise to his name.

CHAPTER FOURTEEN
PIMPS, PROSTIES AND POLITICIANS

Los Angles and Hollywood long have been hotbeds (Did I say that?) of prostitution, though not flagrantly out in the open in recent years, such as smaller cities surrounding Los Angles have had to endure. They don't have brothels, but the streetwalkers are there, busy offering their wares.

San Bernardino County for years had two red light districts where "houses of ill repute" continued to operate in the old fashioned way, with madams, girls, bedrooms, and of course the inevitable pimps who would be off spending the money their women turned over to them.

Prostitution, like society, has its levels of snobbishness. Those at the top serve only the rich and famous. The next level are the higher-priced call girls, while below them are the escort service cocottes and so on, down to the druggies who will solicit a lone male in a parking lot. It all adds up to the same thing,--anything for a buck!

Through the thirties and into the forties San Bernardino essentially was mining and cattle country, then military, with a preponderance of young males in each category to keep the whores occupied.

Some public officials helped the red light districts to stay in business by looking the other way,--for a price. As a result the area in San Bernardino City known as "D" st. was able to operate seven days a week, and the girls could stand in open doorways in skimpy outfits, waving a "come on" to prospective johns driving by, looking over the girls.

The johns, on the other had, could walk into each of the houses and examine the merchandise, like shopping for a pair of comfortable shoes, except for "no touch; not yet!"

At Christmas time these same women would be in the better stores, buying very expensive gifts for their pimps. Nothing was too good for these slimeballs.

Much could be written about these young women and why they chose to do what they were doing.

Red Mountain, in northwestern San Bernardino County, was a different type of red light district. No doubt more than one passerby probably wandered into a café (there were three) and wondered what in the world he had stumbled into when the piano player started to sing a bawdy song, while at the same time a young lady would slide onto the next stool and ask him to buy her a drink.

Yes, this is the way it was, and if the prospective john should turn down her business offer,--a trip to her room, or if it wasn't a busy night, she probably would sit and visit.

Generally the girls had little to do for most of the month. The place was anything but lively. They welcomed any kind of change, even a chance to talk with strangers.

During one such conversation a personable and intelligent young lady was describing her previous employment before doing what she now was doing. (They rarely use words which are common to their trade.)

Among other things, she said she had been an amanuensis for a legal firm. Just the sound of that word made it ring with importance. How could anyone leave a job like that?

She went on to say that she became bored and was looking for more excitement. Well, there was nothing exciting about a dying old mining town tucked away in the empty desert. Different, perhaps, especially for a woman who was used to city life. However, Red Mountain offered a combo getaway for the girls when the heat was on in Los Angeles or Hollywood.

Amanuensis means, basically, the ability to take dictation in which unusual words such as legal or medical terms are employed. Oh, well, I guess in love-making very little needs to be said, except for grunts and groans.

Red light districts couldn't exist without cooperation from authorities, obviously. The business can't be hidden; it has to be right out in the open where everyone can see it.

One day in mid-December the District Attorney stopped by the old Victorville Sheriff's Office, accompanied by his wife, and chatted for a few minutes. In the course of the conversation he told us he was on his way to Red Mountain. After he left I asked Deputy Zeke Eblen why would our DA be going there. Had his wife not been along I would have assumed the old rascal was on his way to visit with one of the girls. "Heck," replied Zeke, "He is on his way to collect his Christmas gifts."

"Gifts?" I said, even though I thought I knew what he meant. "Yeah. You know. A case of booze and maybe a hundred dollars from each of those three joints up there."

It is truly amazing how naïve we, the public, are in such matters. We refuse to believe local politicians are capable of doing such things.

Up to that time the politicians, like the DA, did their own collecting, but soon they were using bagmen, just like Los Angeles. A not-too-smart green and mean deputy was sent to Red Mountain to be a resident officer. In my opinion he should not have been on the force at all, much less to be far away, on his own, without supervision.

To illustrate my point, I should mention an incident which took place a few weeks before his new assignment.

A call had come in from the Harvey House at the S.F.R.R. depot in Barstow, requesting a deputy. A hobo was making a nuisance of himself there. Two deputies responded, one being our friend whom I shall call John.

They collared the bum but he chose to physically resist being taken off to jail.

In return for his struggles he received a hefty blow to the head from John's nightstick. This was uncalled for, but to make matters worse, the blow had been so stout the club broke in two, with the loose end flying off, hitting the other deputy in the face, breaking and bloodying his nose.

Of course I had to turn to Zeke for an explanation. What could such a lamebrain lawman do in a place like that?

"Not much, really," said Zeke, "He's being sent there to count the towels!" Translation: Keeping tabs on the volume of business and being the bagman. A bagman is slang for one who collects money for racketeers (and crooked politicians).

Nevertheless, as the population increased the old ways of life would give way, just as the Indians had been crowded out in their time. Eventually honest lawmen would be elected who believed in law and order. Prostitution will never go away, but bribery of public officials should not be tolerated, nor should red light districts return anywhere in the USA. The price they generate in other crimes and drugs is far too costly to bear.

CHAPTER FIFTEEN
VICTORVILLE, A WARTIME PEYTON PLACE

History has shown that morality during wartime seems to take a setback, partly because of the uncertainties of survival, the parting of young lovers who must say goodbye, and some reasons which defy explanation.

Police see much more infidelity than the public could imagine, and in a small town most of those who play around are known to the law officers. If a crime is committed because of jealousy or rage, it helps to know who might be a suspect.

What indiscretions these folks commit is their own business, of course, but the information is shared among the lawmen. There is little chance for secrecy in places like Victorville. Boy, if some wives had realized this!

World War One had brought about a new emancipation for women, followed by the flapper and prohibition era of the twenties which probably could be called the beginning of a changing attitude. One older comedian lamented that here we were in the middle of a sexual revolution and he was out of ammunition!

There have been women throughout history who believed in free love, and many made the history books, but in one's own home town there always is the feeling that it is different, a clean and wonderful place in which to live and raise kids.

My idealism soon would be shaken as WWII moved along and George AFB was established. Husbands were overseas, and some wives were in the local bars, drinking too much and caring too little.

While patrolling, we would find them in the back seats of parked cars with strangers, or on the ground in an alley. In one instance we found a couple who couldn't wait any longer, but their car was too small, so they stopped alongside the highway where they rolled out onto the ground to finish what had been started. The trouble was, they were in plain sight of everyone passing by. That never bothered them, however.

War years do strange things to people, and there are very few things which escape the police in a small town.

One of our MP's received a medical discharge because of a most unusual accident. It seems he had found a friendly and obliging woman one night and they went into the alley to see about it but they couldn't find a dry spot. Incidentally, this little alley, only two blocks long, probably saw more strange goings on than any other place in town.

He pulled out a flimsy wooden crate from a dumpster and laid her on it. The box could support her weight but his added weight proved to be too much,

Unfortunately for him, as the box collapsed a large sliver rammed far up into a place no self-respecting sliver should go. But this one had been contaminated with assorted germs and caused a severe infection. Even after days in the hospital the poor guy could hardly walk, and he took an unmerciful razzing. He said the worst of it was, he never got to finish what he had started.

After two months or so it was obvious he couldn't perform his duties and wasn't any better, so was given an honorable discharge, which probably made him eligible for a lifetime pension since his injury was sustained in the line of duty.

Hey, fellas, where is that crate, anyway?

CHAPTER SIXTEEN
VICTORVILLE, A TOUGH LITTLE TOWN

Abilene and Dodge City had earned their reputations as tough western towns at about the time Victorville was still nameless, but during the early nineteen hundreds it was earning a name and a reputation for itself.

It was as western in behavior as any town in the U.S. but without the boothills of the nineteenth century. The Mojave Desert was cattle country, mining country, and even Indian country, though the latter were reduced to a small number who worked on the ranches.

Needles, California, however, still had quite a number of tribesmen who were more or less adapting to the ways of the whites, while the squaws greeted each passenger train at the old railroad station, selling their handmade baskets and other examples of the wonderful handicraft passed down through untold centuries of forebears.

Anyone who has a collection of these artifacts is indeed lucky. The originals were of much better quality than any made today. Some of the earlier baskets were woven so tight they could hold water and could be used to heat liquids by dropping hot rocks into the food being prepared.

By the late thirties cowboys still rode into town but only a few hitching racks remained at the curbsides. An annual rodeo was held in Victorville, next to the railroad tracks, close by the station, and for a couple of days the old west lived again, or so it must have seemed to passengers looking on from a passing train.

Naturally there had to be a cowboy dance on Saturday night, and the old American Legion Hall across from the high school was the best place to have it. It also was a good place and an opportune time to let off steam with a fist fight or two, and it always happened. Had this been bygone days, these easily could have been gunfights. Times may have changed, but human nature rarely does.

World War Two brought more serious crimes to the desert, and more of them. It was at this point I realized I needed the help of informants who could tell me, in effect, who was doing what, and where the evidence might be found.

Informants are not necessarily the bad guys, as is commonly believed. Many people have a knack for picking up bits and pieces of gossip around bars and the like where crooks are prone to brag. This information is passed on to an officer they trust and like. Or, sometimes a young fellow will find he joined a theft gang and is into something he hadn't expected. He needs someone he can trust.

One particular informant I shall always remember was of the latter type. He came to me with a story of a motorcycle theft ring nearby in which his first job with them was to grind the identification numbers off the frames and engines of the stolen bikes, then stamp false numbers in their place.

We watched this operation for a while, then moved in when the whole gang was in the shop, arrested them, and later won convictions in court.

Another informant at a different time came to me with a story I had to doubt. He told me where a Thompson sub-machine gun was hidden.

When I finally had time I drove to the location and found he was telling the truth. Not only was there a Tommy gun but about a thousand rounds of ammunition for it, with many of the boxes being of plain cardboard with U.S. military markings on them.

Then it hit me. I remembered reading a few weeks before that a military base a few hundred miles away had "lost" a sizable number of weapons including several Tommies. This is not unusual, even today, but the losses are not divulged. If gun control should be established in the future, Uncle Sam will become an unwitting supplier of guns for the crooks.

Tommy guns were still in big demand by mobsters and were worth several thousand dollars when they could be bought. Not only could they fire off a lot of rounds quickly, but they had the advantage of being short, which meant a crook could sit in the back seat of a car and blast away from either side or the back window at will,--and they were easy to hide. They were the weapon of choice for the bad guys in those times.

Now I had a sub-machine gun and didn't know what to do with it. I had three choices. If I turned it into higher authority it probably would disappear in someone's gun collection. In any event, it wouldn't remain in the evidence locker for as little as overnight.

Or, if by some chance it became a case for higher authorities to investigate, the thieves who stole it would learn where it was and they could be real mean mobsters who might want to find out who doublecrossed them by making off with the gun, in which case I and my family could be in real danger, and so would my informant.

Neither of these options had any merit, nor would anything be solved with an investigation, which brought me to option number three. I would dispose of it myself.

Before doing so, I decided to keep it for the present and practice shooting a Tommy gun with all that ammunition. Previous to this I had learned to shoot one, but was permitted to shoot only four or five rounds at a time.

Because this weapon is short and rather light, it has a lot of recoil. When used on full automatic, one must lean into it and brace himself, otherwise the muzzle will rise skyward as each bullet is fired. Likewise, beginners will find their finger is frozen to the trigger and won't back off.

For a time I kept that thing and would go out to the open desert to shoot it. The recoil is rather tough on the shoulder, so I would use about fifty cartridges at a time. Anyway, I learned to handle a sub-machine gun, and after seeing what twenty or so bullets would do to a large cardboard box it wasn't hard to picture what could happen to a human being.

After the ammo was gone I cut the gun into a number of chunks and scattered them over the desert, except for one piece, a piece which could never be used again.

Eventually the Tommy gun lost its popularity, giving way to the sawed off shotgun, a weapon which is short, light, deadly, and hardly needs to be aimed. In fact, it can be shot from the hip.

There may be a few who might be critical of the way I handled the matter of the machine gun, but the realities of life often call for some compromise in order to reach the important objective. Reality is reality. I don't intend to be a foolish hero, nor do I intend to be a fool.

Informants come in all shapes, sizes, and ages. Some of our best are little kids who were in the family car when daddy ran off the road and tore up the front end. Dad would tell us some heroic story about how he swerved to avoid a dog and the dog ran off unharmed.

When I had a chance I would get the boy aside and say, "Do you know what happened?" "Yes," the lad might say, "Dad was reaching over to adjust the radio and he didn't watch where he was going."

Well, out of the mouths of babes----!

September 26, 1946. Big train wreck just south of the Oro Grande Bridge, near Los Angeles Bureau of Power and Light Switching Station. Six killed, fifty or more injured. Eleven cars wrecked. Traffic so heavy on Highway 66 I had to direct traffic near the scene.

Buzz Banks, a brand new CHP officer wearing a brand new CHP motorcycle uniform. About to move to Victorville from his home behind him in San Bernardino, ready to start a new career.

CHAPTER SEVENTEEN
A POLICE OFFICER'S JOB IS LIKE NO OTHER

Officers when making an arrest may use no more force than necessary, but how much resistance should he have to fight off, on a give and take basis?

Almost nothing has been said about law enforcement in the U.S. before the wild wild west came along. From that time Bat Masterson, Wyatt Earp, Ike Clanton and Billy the Kid started legends ranging from dime novels to movies, radio, and television. Along the way every enforcement type of activity has been glamorized, ridiculed, condemned, praised, and on rare occasions has been reported truthfully and factually.

Often the police are criticized for using too much force in some arrests, but if greater force is needed to do the job, that force must be applied. When the officers lose control, the bad guys seem to go berserk, even to the extreme of going on a killing spree.

Some officers in time give up the tough part of the job because they find they are not equal to it. They take the easy way out, seeing nothing and hearing nothing during the rest of their career, making no felony arrests or anything which might result in a court trial. The best they can do is to write violations for such things as finding someone driving with one headlight out. They feel uncomfortable in court on the witness stand, where they are put on trial by the defense attorney. This can be trying and exasperating.

Working law enforcement is like walking on quicksand; the ground is always changing under us because of changing laws. As a result, twenty years is long enough to be a peace officer. Many years ago Wyatt Earp found he had outlasted his time and ended up on the wanted list he once enforced. A recent Los Angeles chief of police found himself removed from office because his concepts were considered outdated.

By 1940 the rules covering police procedures had tightened up considerably, though officers still were permitted to think and to act as individuals, and this is as it should be, so long as they stay within the law.

Many times I have been asked why I chose police work and the California Highway Patrol when there were other choices. Simple. I did not want a nine to five job, nor to be tied to a desk. My life to that time had always been outdoors, with occasional moments of exciting experiences added for good measure. I was looking for a lifetime of the same, and the CHP had it all. When later I was assigned as a resident officer where I had the desert to the front and my San Bernardino mountains at my back, fortune truly had smiled on me.

Nothing seemed impossible. Nothing was too tough. I thought I was ready for anything. High speed pursuits were fun, accident investigations were interesting and interrogations were challenging. Every experience was something new for me.

When I checked in at Victorville I increased the CHP crew by one hundred percent, becoming the second officer. Later we grew to four, then down to three, then two, and finally only one,--me. The armed services were taking my partners away to serve in World War Two.

War demands were shrinking the force of deputies also, thus we totaled so few lawmen there was only one thing to do,--we helped each other. They came to help me at accident scenes, while I rolled to assist at murders, family fights, bar brawls, or whatever came along.

Every day seemed to bring something unusual. I found there was a lot for me to learn, such as controlling a motorcycle at ninety miles per hour in a strong wind on a gravel-covered road. Or getting out of a warm bed at two a.m., working up a sweat trying to kickstart an obstinate motorcycle, then trying to avoid freezing to death in five degree weather as I sped through the night to reach an accident scene. We had no decent ambulance backup, we provided first aid, and to save lives it was our duty to get to the victims as quickly as we could. Our winters were much colder years ago, which made it tough for the injured and for us.

For about a year we used motorcycles before we could convince headquarters of the need for a car. They finally gave us a heaterless 1941 Ford but we could only use it at night. It, too, had tricks of its own. In the usual strong desert winds it wouldn't steer very well. Added to that, it handled badly at high speeds because of improper suspension. On every bump in the road, and old Highway #66 had many, all four wheels would leave the pavement. While airborne the wind would turn us sideways about ten degrees. After the first three leaps we knew how much we would be blown off course and would turn the steering wheel accordingly before landing. It was a constant challenge to see if we could stay right side up.

Invariably the speeder I had been chasing would be mad at himself for being caught. They always thought they were too alert for that and wondered where I came from. Well, try this: I came out of the nowhere into the here!

Probably the most important thing I had to learn was how essential it was to maintain control in all contacts at all times. This is something liberals don't understand. Most contacts are unimportant, though now and then things can suddenly become grim. Many officers have lost their lives at such times. Moreover, other lives often are at stake.

Several years ago a CHP officer stopped to help a wrong way driver at Cajon Summit. The subject was a wanted criminal who thought he was about to be arrested. He waited until the officer was at a momentary disadvantage, then seized the officer's holstered pistol and killed him. He jumped into the patrol car and roared off down the hill. Before it was over he also killed a deputy sheriff and a luckless service station attendant who was talking on the telephone, all within the space of five minutes. Bad things almost always happen when the officer loses control, whether the subject is an individual or a riot is in the making.

Recent riots have proved several things. One is that they can happen at any time and, two, they should be stopped at the very beginning before lots of innocent people get hurt or killed. Potential rioters have already lost common sense and are a loaded gun, waiting for something to pull the trigger. They are past listening to reason

Many things we officers had to do in the forties would not be tolerated today, but one thing will always be true,--we were in a better position to protect the public than is the case today. Lawmen are hired to protect people and property. This cannot be done when they are so restricted they have no authority to act in a forceful manner when force is called for but must sit and wait for higher authority to give permission. A delay of two seconds can be one second too many.

The old Scott's Café Niteball Team, during World War Two, usually referred to as "The Tired Old Men" because we had not been drafted. I am the one seated at the left.

I sure would like to hear from any of my team mates who still are alive. The guys in the picture are, back row, left to right, L.McElvain, Dan Greenwood, Pete Anthony, Paul Dewitt, Carl Thrasher, Jack Redden, Bob Angel; front row, Buzz Banks, Ray Ramirez, Bob Orrantia, Wayne Green, Miles Crafton. Not present were Bob Mullen and Paul Scott – Scott's Café Owner. Louie Roehrig worked for the LABP&L and for a time owned the bar, pool, & motel where Gary and Sue Scissel lived and owned just below the Oro Grande Bridge.

CHAPTER EIGHTEEN
DEATH ON A SUMMER DAY

Few occupations offer the kinds of challenges and the variety of problems which are faced by police officers. No two days ever are the same, no two situations are identical. Many contacts are comical, helping to relieve some of the stress which goes with the job, while others are so terribly tragic they become forever imbedded in our memory.

Reporting for duty may be fairly routine, but nothing else will be. The public literally will dictate what we will experience during our shift. We may have a reasonably calm day, or at some moment, perhaps only a split second, we will be faced with a life or death decision. We must think and take action instantly, but our decision may take weeks of argument in a court of law.

While on patrol one warm sunny afternoon in 1955 I was working solo, and I mean solo. No other CHP unit was within forty miles, nor were sheriffs' units nearer than several miles. My radio, which had been relatively silent, suddenly put out a call that a shot had been fired at the housing by George Air Force Base and the subject had fled in his car. A brief description of the car followed, driven by a young adult male, no other description.

I was not far from the Base so I cruised the area, looking for the vehicle. Shortly I spotted it, apparently stuck in the sand about two hundred yards out in the desert west of Highway #395.

I promptly radioed my location and that I had found the car and was advised some deputies were on the way. About this same moment I heard a gunshot but saw no one who could have fired it nor anything to be shot at, except possibly at me.

Assuming there might be more shots, I quickly drove out of range, then circled around and with a small hill for cover I drove back on a dirt road which he must have traveled from the other direction.

At the east edge of the hill the subject was finally seen to my right, sitting with his back pressed against a Joshua tree, holding a small nickel-plated revolver in both hands, the muzzle shoved into his chest. There was no other choice for me but to jump out of the patrol car, take cover behind it, and draw my own pistol.

Too often a person intent upon committing suicide will threaten an officer rather than to shoot himself. Because he was only twelve feet away, the best thing for both of us was for me to steady my elbows on the car hood and keep aiming my firearm on his pistol. Should he turn it toward me I would have no choice but to shoot it out of his hand. At least we both would be alive.

For a time that seemed ages I talked to him, trying to dissuade him. I didn't know what had led him to this, but used the theme that nothing was so bad it could not be solved, and similar thoughts. It seemed I might be getting through to him.

Within minutes three deputies arrived but there was little they could do, although one slipped around out of sight and quickly returned to our right, behind and well back of the subject. From there he was trying to get close enough to knock the pistol away, though I had my doubts this could succeed.

Another two minutes passed before two MP's and their captain arrived. He immediately took over and from about twenty feet away he started talking to the young fellow whom they knew to be a GI from the Base.

He started pursuing the buddy buddy routine of the military, mutual problems, and more of the same. It was only making matters worse, as all seemed to realize. No one said a word. It was obvious this lad was fed up and blaming the military for his problems.

Suddenly the young man finally spoke. Calling out, he said, "Captain, can you count to five?" The captain replied, "Yes."

"Oke, go ahead and count to five," was the response, and the captain started counting slowly, with we six listening, aghast, for we knew what was coming, but the captain was not one of the most astute men I have ever met and continued his count, "—, two, three, four, five."

At the count of five the poor GI said, "five. That's it!" and pressed the trigger with his thumb, the muzzle of his pistol still thrust into his chest.

With only twelve feet separating the two of us, it all seemed like slow motion. At the sound of the shot his first expression was one of surprise, as though he didn't expect to feel the pain of the bullet. This was instantly followed by a grimace of agony, then blankness, all in about one second during which he remained seated upright. In another moment he slumped forward, a living human being no more.

In a strange way, somehow, it was like a tableau in a macabre play; the empty desert, a black raven or two wheeling overhead, and seven men standing by in horrified silence, watching a man take his own life.

After the military police had concluded their initial investigation we were told what probably was a primary cause for this suicide. The young man had just been told his wife was leaving him for another man. She probably had her reasons, but the husband blamed all his troubles on the military and wasn't thinking very straight. Also, he probably thought that by killing himself he was "getting even" with his wife, making her have remorse. They found only three empty casings in his pistol. He had saved the last bullet for himself.

I have often wondered how others, finding themselves in my position, would handle the matter. Any suggestions? Was there something I could have done to stop this lad from taking his own life? After the MP's arrived, the matter was out of my hands.   But for that, I could be blaming myself.

Where the young airman committed suicide. He was seated against the Joshua tree as demonstrated by the MP. My patrol unit was parked in approximately the spot as the car at the right.

CHAPTER NINETEEN
WE LOSE A FINE YOUNG OFFICER

No arrest is "routine," whether it is nothing more than stopping a motorist for speeding or driving with no tail lights. In fact, it is a time when officers are most apt to get careless.

One night we heard a frantic call coming over the California Highway Patrol radio frequency. We could not recognize the voice, and the language did not follow radio procedure. Whoever was talking was almost incoherent. He said he was in a parked CHP car and an officer was dead on the pavement and would someone hurry up and help him.

Within minutes I was there, and already several onlookers had stopped. The officer's patrol car was parked, lights on, motor off. Our officer's body was lying on the pavement fairly close to the dirt shoulder. He had been shot once in the heart on once through the head.

By examining the scene it was determined the officer had stopped an unknown motorist, most likely for speeding, had pulled up a few feet back of the subject vehicle which had stopped with all four wheels on the dirt shoulder.

Two footprints about midway of the tire tracks, at right angle to the tracks, indicated the killer had opened the door on the driver's side, put his feet on the ground, and awaited the officer who by that time was approaching on foot. The subject evidently held a pistol hidden behind his right thigh and when our officer was approximately at the left rear fender, so close as to be an easy target, the man simply raised the gun and pulled the trigger, putting the bullet through the officer's left shirt pocket where it continued through the heart and chest.

Not satisfied with that shot, the shooter fired at the dead man's head but missed, the bullet gouging the pavement in a near miss. He then stooped over, fired one more time with the pistol's muzzle almost against the left temple of the downed body. This bullet passed through the head and nicked the pavement before ricocheting into the distance.

Then the killer jumped back into his car and headed north to Victorville where he abandoned his stolen vehicle by the bowling alley, stole another, and headed back south, driving right by the murder scene which by that time was loaded with officers and deputies.

We soon found the subject vehicle, its tire treads matching the tire prints found in the dirt. A license check was run through channels and the report showed it had been stolen in Riverside.

Fingerprints from the interior proved to be those of an ex-con. Further investigation indicated he had robbed a super market in Riverside about thirty minutes before the fatal shooting.

Within twenty-four hours he was in custody. At first he was going to shoot it out with the SWAT team rather than surrender. They had to promise him they would not harm him.

Later he reenacted the shooting in front of TV cameras at the scene. Everything he did was exactly as we had concluded in our investigation.

Eventually he went to the gas chamber, but that could not bring back the life of a fine young officer who had not followed the guidelines for approaching a violator. We knew this conclusively because his citation book lay by his left hand, his flashlight by the right hand. The proper way is to hold the flashlight in the left hand, the citation book tucked under the left arm, and the right hand just above the officer's firearm. Left handers will have to do this from their side. In either case there are other things he must do to protect himself, but he always must be on his guard. The criminal knows what he wants to do and is watching for his chance to go into action.

A strange part of this story was added by a girl friend who told investigators that she, the killer, and a man friend of his had driven out toward Death Valley just a few weeks earlier and engaged in target practice at the roadside. She said her boyfriend had pulled out a pistol and shot several rounds into a Joshua tree.

She was able to lead a team of deputies to the scene, pointed out the tree, and the officers dug out several bullets. Laboratory tests proved they were identical to the bullet found in our officer's chest.

Criminals always think they are too smart to get caught, but they make dumb mistakes—and they do get caught.

1942 Jackie Brown, son of Deputy Sheriff in charge of the Victorville sub-station, Jack Brown, sitting astride my old CHP "seventy-four" Harley Davidson motorcycle.
He is now the top man at the huge Stater Brothers Grocery chain. His mom is on the 1994-95 San Bernardino County Grand Jury!

CHAPTER TWENTY
LUCK STILL CONTROLS WHETHER WE LIVE OR DIE

Officers deal with dangerous people when on duty, and often when not on duty. Somehow, the bad guys seem to sense our official status even when we are out of uniform and just having a good time.

One day in late spring of 1942 Jack Brown, the deputy in charge of the Victorville sheriff's office, invited a member of the military police, Bill Newberry, and me to accompany him out to the Giant Rock airport, near Twentynine Palms.

We gladly accepted and off we went, for a ride of about fifty miles each way. Riding with us was Jack's little son, known by all of us as Jackie Brown, only four years old.

On the way we were told that the resident of the airport was a man by the name of Frank Kritzer, purportedly the sole owner. His airport was nothing more that a long landing strip for any private planes and not an official airport.

World War Two was now our problem. Strange things were going on in the desert near the Giant Rock and nearby Twentynine Palms. Flares had been set off on mountain tops, dynamite had been stolen from mining companies, and worse, unintelligible shortwave radio transmissions had been heard.

Many stories have been told about Frank, understandably, because he was a mystery man of the desert. One tale claimed he was a deserter from the German army during World War One who had fled to the U.S. and eventually came west. An added legend had it that the Nazis would forgive him and let him return after the war if he would be a "nuisance spy" for them by setting off flairs and sending gibberish on the special radio they provided. This would tie up FBI investigators while real spies infiltrated the U.S.

How he found the Giant Rock and took it over could be another strange story. It appears that some miner of an earlier time had dug or at least enlarged a big hole under the rock and lived there like a hermit while he prospected. This entire region is full of weird accounts of Indian manhunts, feuds, and shootings, so one more was not unusual.

Upon our approach we could see this huge and somewhat rounded rock standing by itself next to a mountain rising rather abruptly at its westerly edge. A long, long wire let upward from the rock and disappeared over a ridge of the hill.

Surrounding the rock on the other three sides was a large cleared area, with a rifle target keeping a lonely vigil about a hundred yards to the east.

Facing east at ground level was a small screened opening in the face of the rock, with a door in the middle. At the doorway a man seemed to have been expecting us, for he quickly appeared without our needing to knock.

He was a dour-looking man at first, but when he saw little Jackie he appeared to soften up. We are certain he felt we meant him no harm or we would not have brought along a small child.

We introduced ourselves and indicated we were simply interested in his unusual home under that rock. He visibly warmed up to us and invited us into his home.

Upon entering the screened room, which was little more than a landing for a stairway which led downward to the left, turned right about midway where the rock was a wall in front of our faces, then down to the floor. This proved to serve two rooms, a kitchen to our left and a living room to our right. Facing us in this room was a fireplace with a mantel above. To the left of this was a shelf secured to the rock about six feet above the floor. On this shelf was a large and powerful radio, obviously capable of receiving shortwave signals, though he said he needed a good radio and a good antenna to get any reception so far from the stations. It must have had a transmitter, but I did not see one.

On the mantel was a very large case such as those used for binoculars, except that this was built to take the old fashioned double telescope. Protruding from its top was a handle which looked for all the world like the handle of a dynamite plunger. A few months later three Riverside County deputies found out the hard way that it was exactly that.

Another rather large room adjoined the living area but was connected only by a sizable window-like opening. This arrangement created a natural form of air conditioning because one side of the rock would be in the shade while the opposite side was in the sun, thus causing the cooler air to move in.

Frank was proud of what he had accomplished with the place and answered our questions. Of course we were careful not to ask pointed ones. We were there to use our eyes.

It was apparent that Frank was a secretive man who answered only in general terms. He was about fifty-seven, lean but strong, standing about six feet tall and would weigh about a hundred and sixty-five pounds. His speech had a definite Germanic accent.

He left us for a few minutes to take care of something and his absence undoubtedly saved the lives of the three deputies who followed us a month or so later.

During this absence little Jackie's feet became tangled in a wire. Big Jack went over to him and removed the entanglement and we thought nothing of it, but somewhere that wire had pulled loose, unknown to us.

Two months later three Riverside deputies were investigating the theft of explosives which had occurred in their county. They decided to pay Frank a visit to question him. At this point their stories are confused, but they must have scared him into thinking they were about to take him to jail. He lived free and intended to stay free or die.

He walked over to the mantel, took down the binocular case, hung it by its straps so it rested against his chest, and pushed the plunger. Some say he touched two wires together. Either way, there were at least three sticks of dynamite in that case., The resulting explosion blew him in half, except for a shred of skin, while a deputy who was near the door was blown out into the yard, losing most of his clothing in the blast.

Apparently the other two men were close to the further walls and survived, but one was hurt rather severely.

All three survived and were able to get help, but they never learned a little boy had saved their lives. If they read this, it may come as new to them. A later inspection of the rooms disclosed two stashes of wired dynamite which never exploded, but they would have, had not our little Jackie tripped on a wire along the floor. There was enough explosive to blow that rock to pieces.

Later the Giant Rock Airport allegedly became the home for wandering UFO's, while that little boy grew up, went on to college, and became president and chairman of the board of the huge Stater Brothers Market chain of fine supermarkets throughout Southern California. His name today is Jack Brown.

CHAPTER TWENTY-ONE
YOUNG OFFICERS CAN BE TOO YOUNG

Breaking in young rookies often present strange problems for their sergeants and training officers.

One such officer, Joe, was irrepressible. He had not matured enough to start wearing a badge, but had managed somehow to get by the oral interview board which had tested him before he could join the California Highway Patrol.

Most of his transgressions had been rather juvenile and had not hurt anyone except, perhaps, himself. One of these incidents was when he responded to an accident call given to another officer, but he wanted to create some excitement for himself, so he turned on the red light on his motorcycle and took off at high speed, without authorization to do so.

His trouble started where the road curved. He still was a green kid with little biker experience to prepare him for high speed and had been warned to take it easy.

After rounding the first curve he thought he was pretty good so he opened up the throttle some more, but the next curve was meaner and he didn't know how to lean into it. His bike shot off the road and into space, landing some hundred feet beyond. Joe was only slightly hurt, but the motorcycle wasn't so lucky.

There was no official reprimand because his injury was felt to be sufficient, but this did not mean he had matured. Far from it! Soon he was to outdo himself.

Late one evening a car containing two men went off the road and down the bank by the Highway #18 bridge, throwing out the two occupants and rolling to a stop just short of the railroad tracks.

Joe and a sheriff's deputy hastened to the scene and clambered down the steep bank to the two victims who were lying several feet apart. The deputy leaned over one of them and saw that the man definitely was dead, so he called out to Joe, who was kneeling beside the other victim, "Joe, this one is dead. How about that one, is he dead, too?"

Unknown to any of us, Joe had taken a blank starter pistol off some crook a week or so before but had said nothing to any of us about it. He was waiting for a chance to pull off a practical joke, and now the time had come.

He leaned more closely over the second victim, already dead, put the blank pistol seemingly, but not actually, at the subject's head. The deputy couldn't see all this in the dark, but what he did hear was, "No, he's not dead!" Then the deputy heard a pistol shot when Joe pulled the trigger and yelled, "But he is now!" The deputy had momentary heart failure until he realized he had been had.

Nowadays an officer could be fired for that, but this was a different time and almost as much a different world as the days of Billy the Kid. Nothing changes so much in this universe as does the ground upon which a policeman walks.

CHAPTER TWENTY-TWO
WHEN LUCK RUNS OUT ON OLD
U.S. HIGHWAY #66

Someone once said, "If I didn't have bad luck, I wouldn't have any luck at all!" But there are times for some people when this is all too prophetic—and fatal.

Close to midnight a family of five were headed for their home near Los Angeles after a trip east to visit family and friends. The return trip had been marred by a series of breakdowns and costly repairs. Bad luck had been dogging them all the way back to California.

They were broke, with only four dollars left and still more than one hundred miles from home. For the last several hundred miles they had been sleeping in the car when they could, trying to stretch their last few dollars.

As they neared Victorville, a drunk seventeen-year old driver was headed their way, bringing with him their final piece of misfortune, -- and his, too.

It happened on a slight curve which the other vehicle straightened out, heading across the road and straight at this poor man and his family who already had suffered so much bad luck

His wife and little ones were sound asleep, and probably never knew what happened, but he was wide awake on a two-lane roadway without shoulders, hoping to get home without further trouble.

Suddenly he saw a pair of headlights coming straight at him, on his side of the road. The other driver had driven across a slight curve and crossed into his lane. There was no time to take evasive action, and nowhere to go if he could. In the resulting crash all six were killed outright.

The victim's car was completely crushed, with the left and right sides mashed together. The speedometer on the violator's car was stuck at seventy-four miles per hours.

I often have thought about that accident; it had the pathetic elements of repeated bad luck which make it different from most.

What were his final thoughts, after all the bad luck this man and suffered? He knew the two cars were about to crash and he was totally helpless to avoid it. Could he and his family survive? What else could possibly happen? All he possibly could hope for was a last moment miracle.

An old wives' tale says that bad luck always comes in threes. What do you think? How many did this man have?

Feb. 26, 1949. This is an interior of CHP Patrol vehicle where two CHP officers were badly injured. A wrong-way DUI driver hit them head on. They were in pursuit of a different car at the time. Their bodies did the damage seen here. The driver eventually returned to duty, the other was unable to serve again on the patrol. This was before seat belts and clearly shows why they should be worn today.

CHAPTER TWENTY-THREE
THE AGONY OF FEARING THE WORST

Life for a traffic officer is a veritable host of different experiences ranging from excitement to humor, and to the pathos suffered by others. It is a fine career for those who prefer the outdoors and do not want to be cooped up in an office with a nine to five sort of job.

An officer must be able to think for himself, be in command of his emotions, yet empathize with those who are traumatized by the sudden loss of loved ones. We see far too much of this.

So many times we are called to an accident scene where kids or loved ones have been seriously hurt or killed and we have to tell white lies to other badly injured victims, telling them everyone else is ok and have be sent on for checkup. I don't like to tell lies, but a fib such as this is vital. It is imperative that injured folks are under a doctor's care before they learn the awful truth, otherwise they can, and have, gone into fatal shock. At such a time the officer must act perfectly cheerful and professional.

Often there are occasions when we or the coroner have to be the bearer of tragic news to the family waiting at home. One of the most pathetic responses I ever had experienced came when Deputy County Coroner Ed Doyle and I delivered such a message to a distraught mother of a youngster who had not returned home on schedule.

About one A.M. a two-car collision occurred just north of Victorville near the Los Angeles Bureau of Power and Light switching station on Old Highway 66 when a vehicle carrying two men crossed over the centerline, smashing into another car with four people aboard, two adults and two little girls. All six were killed instantly and the two autos looked like one pile of twisted metal.

We were able to identify five of the six, but a little girl of about seven had no identification whatsoever. We only knew she belonged to someone other than the two adults.

Much precious time was lost in waking neighbors of the deceased until we finally got a lead which took us to a trailer park in Adelanto, past four o'clock in the morning.

We had no space number, but a light was shining from a window in one trailer, and we reasoned that must be the one.

Ed knocked on the door while I stood back a distance. We long ago learned that when people see an officer at their door they immediately think the worst.

A fully dressed and rather overweight woman of about thirty or so appeared in the doorway. She looked beyond Ed and saw me, whereupon she threw her arms upward, as though in appeal to God and cried out, "Don't tell me she's dead! Don't tell me she's dead!" and fell back into the room, dropping into a large chair where she must have been sitting throughout the night, worrying and fearing the worst.

There was so little that Ed or I could say except to ask if she would like to get a doctor. She was in shock so deep there were no tears, but she was able to ask us to call the Air Force hospital.

We stayed with her until the medics arrived and took her back with them. We later learned they knew her well because of her poor health, that the little girl was her only child and she might be unable to have another. Also she had lost her father in a traffic accident only a year earlier.

It is very doubtful anyone could have told her of this accident prior to our knock at her door. She could only await her daughter's return. After midnight the worry must have become premonition. Had we arrived with her child those fears would have vanished; without her the mother knew the terrible truth before a single word was spoken.

Even today, almost forty years later, I still share this mother's grief. That poor, poor woman.

CHAPTER TWENTY-FOUR
SPIES IN THE OUTHOUSE

During the early years of World War II the American people were seeing German spies everywhere in every state, and literally behind the bushes. Everyone was understandably nervous. As each sighting was reported it was promptly investigated.

Such a report was phoned in to the old Victorville Sheriffs' Office from Lucerne Valley one day, the caller stating that an elderly couple was in his store, Ewings' Desert Trading Post, to report that German spies were then hiding on their property, some distance out in the desert.

Captain Zeke Eblen, the deputy in charge, took the message and promptly drove the twenty-three miles to the store where he talked with Art Ewing who advised him the couple were a little wacky but seemed quite excited about the spies. After getting directions at the store Zeke easily found the property where the spies were said to be hiding. The site proved to be a tiny desert homestead with the usual small shack needed to qualify for claiming title, and the usual one-holer outhouse out back.

As Zeke stepped across the threshold, his eyes quickly roved the single room, taking in its contents which consisted of one bed, a wood cook stove, three kitchen chairs and a wooden table. Off in a corner was a mess of soiled utensils hiding a semblance of a sink. There were no pets, no large animals outside, not even a small garden.

After they all had introduced themselves the three spent several minutes in small talk, while Zeke sized them up. It began to look like Art Ewing had made a correct assessment.

Another few minutes were needed for Zeke to obtain the preliminary data needed in all investigations. He had to hold his notebook on his lap because the table was too cluttered to use, the clutter consisting of family belongings, other odds and ends, plus a large pumpkin in the center, as though its purpose was to be a centerpiece.

Finally he was ready with the important question, "Can you tell me where I might find these spies?" "Oh," they both said as one, "They are in the outhouse!" "Really? Are you sure? Have you seen them there?" "Oh, my goodness no. We can't see them, but we hear their voices all the time, coming up from down below." With that remark the old lady added as an afterthought, "I think I'll make a pumpkin pie!" Putting action to the words she grabbed the pumpkin, dropped it on the floor at her feet and stomped it open. The, reaching down, she picked up the pieces and tossed them into one of the cooking pots.

There was little else to say except "Goodbye." On his way out, Zeke took his flashlight, walked over to the outhouse, peered down into the pit below, but saw nothing. Nothing suspicious, that is. His final report stated, "I visited the alleged spy scene, found no evidence of spies, but did find evidence of foul play!" The case of the "Outhouse Mystery" was closed. Nothing more was ever heard from below. Well, almost nothing.

Some of the Military Police from the air base. A special deputy is on the left. I am at the front right. 7th St. is behind us, with the sheriff's office just off to the left. These men and others certainly were a big help to all of us.

CHAPTER TWENTY-FIVE
WHO DAT SAY "WHO DAT" WHEN I SAY "WHO DAT?"

Police work isn't always deadly serious. In fact, there are far more humorous incidents occurring that one might expect from enforcing the law. Every day at least one of us would have a funny experience we would relate to the others.

One such incident originated here in Victorville and became a "gag" story which went all over the country, with different towns given the credit.

Across the railroad tracks is an area known as "E" St., occupied during WWII mostly by Latino and black folks. One block was the little business section, with an alley to the rear. None of this part of town was very well lit, and the alley at night was total blackness.

One night a call came in stating that someone was seen trying to break into the grocery store. Two MP's accompanied one deputy to the location where it was decided the deputy would cover the front, while the MP's would enter the alley from each end and they would converge upon the store.

As the MP's were nearing each other they heard a slight metallic thump coming from the darkness where the trash cans were kept. A few minutes later they returned to the sheriff's car with a subject in tow and laughing.

When asked what was so funny, on of them had this to say about his partner: "We both heard this noise but we couldn't see a thing back in that trash, so Sam calls out, 'Who dat?' and a voice comes back from among the cans, saying in reply, 'Who dat?'. Then Sam, here yells out in a loud and commanding voice, "Who dat say Who dat when Ah say "Who dat?' Well, the guy gives up and comes out and we grab him." Needless to say, the Military Police for the military air base (Now George Air Force Base) were great fellows and they gave us enormous support during those years when were so short on manpower.

CHAPTER TWENTY-SIX
SURE AND IT'S NOT WHAT I MEANT

Among my duties during WWII was serving as a driver's license examiner. There was no DMV office in the entire Mojave desert, so, as a matter of convenience to desert residents, and to help them save their gasoline coupons, Walt Terry in Barstow and I in Victorville volunteered to add this duty to our regular activities. Thus, once each month one or the other of us would do this at Needles, Barstow, Trona, and Victorville.

New jobs always seem to be a case of learning what to do and by our mistakes, learning what not to do. This one taught me the value of saying exactly what we want the other person to do, in clear and understandable language,

One day at Barstow I had been having a long and trying morning without letup, except for lunch. By midafternoon there were only two or three applicants left, giving me the feeling I could relax a bit by using a little whimsy if the right sort of applicant showed up.

The very next man who came in appeared to be a man who liked a joke, so I kidded with him a bit when I told him he had passed the True-False test. Next I would need his thumb print on his application form, but instead of telling him exactly what I wanted in good English, I asked him to show me his "Paddy-whacker." I was certain he would be familiar with this old Irish word which once meant the hand used to whack an Irish baby's behind, or to form paddycakes in kid's games.

He gave me a funny look, turned sideways a bit, and reached for his fly. Luckily there were only the two of us in the room at the time.

"Hey," I said, "what are you doing? I asked for your paddywhacker,--your right hand!"

"Oh, my gosh, I thought you said you wanted to see my tallywhacker. I wondered what that had to do with getting a driver's license!"

"Nope," I replied, "I don't think it would fingerprint very good."

We both laughed. He was a good sport, surrendered his thumb for printing, and left in a very happy mood, holding a nice new four-year driver's license in his—paddywacker.

CHAPTER TWENTY-SEVEN
ONLOOKERS CAN BE PROBLEMS

Curiosity seekers are attracted to traffic accidents, and nobody has figured out just why. Many explanations have been offered, but seeing the blood, the injured, the dead can hardly be defined as pleasant. Morbidity seems to be the guiding impulse.

Sometimes these onlookers gather in such numbers as to interfere with the conduct of the investigation. There have been times when I have had to hold up my citation book in front of them and tell them they are in our way and must leave or be cited for such interference. Often another group would appear, only to be told the same thing. I never had to write anyone a ticket, but some needed a reminder.

There are officers who, to some extent, wish that such people would mind their own business. One officer I can recall had a rather macabre sense of humor he would use when he felt a stranger was intruding a bit too much.

One morning there was a one-car rollover near Helendale, with only one person involved who, sadly, was decapitated. The officer, whom I shall call Paul, was taking measurements needed for his report, when a passerby stopped and stepped out of his car to look over the scene.

Suddenly he saw the headless body lying about a hundred feet from the road. He called over to Paul, "Where's the man's head?" Paul looked up from his report and replied in a low and solemn tone, "You're standing on it!" The man looked down, and there in a bush closeby his feet was a grizzly sight, and one which was too strong for the gentleman's stomach. As soon as he recovered, he beat a hasty retreat.

Just at the end of our shift a call came in reporting a one car rollover on the Palmdale Road near the L.A. County line on one of the big curves at that point. The subject vehicle had left the road, rolled two or three times, finally ejected the driver, fatally, and came to a stop, upside down. We had to await the coroner in those days, so we spent a miserable few hours sitting in the patrol car in the dark. We should have had a couple of books to read.

Darkness was one blessing, at least, because passing motorists cold not see the wreck out in the desert, nor the body lying below the engine compartment. The hood had been torn off, the dead man was facing up, and one arm was reaching upward toward the carburetor.

Finally came the dawn and visibility, bringing with it our first visitor. He stopped, came over, saw the body in its peculiar position, and asked Paul, "Is he dead?" Paul was cold, tired, and hungry. He looked at the guy for a long moment before replying, "Naw. He's working on his car!" This ended further conversation. Subject departed.

Finally the coroner arrived and in effect said what we already knew, "Yep, he's dead," adding, "I'll check your report back in town at a restaurant!"

CHAPTER TWENTY-EIGHT
ALIBIS

Officers hear every conceivable alibi for the wrongdoer's misdeeds. Speeders probably offer the most excuses, such as, "I was speeding to get to town before I ran out of gas." Or, "I was in a hurry to get to a restroom." Or, how about this one? "I was watching my mirror real close! Where in the Hell did YOU come from?"

Then there was the Latino I had stopped for speeding. He was mad at be because he thought I was picking on Mexicans, not stopping to think that during my pursuit I had no idea who or what was driving the car I was clocking. It could have been a gorilla, for all I knew. What he also didn't know was that I had many friends among all races, and my only concern was to do my job. There is no need to play favorites.

As I was writing out the ticket his anger was growing and his face puffed out with his efforts to restrain himself. I actually felt sorry for him, seeing him become so distraught. I finished the ticket, passed it over for his signature, showed him where to sign his agreement to appear in court, and handed him my pencil. At this point he was livid. With a flourish which almost tore the paper in two, he signed his name. While literally exploding with resentment he said, "The next Goddam time I come these way, I don't come at all." Oh, well, citations aren't intended to make friends.

Even illegal parking draws alibis. People make them up before they have a chance to think how ridiculous the excuse will sound. One such remark was made by a man who parked at the intersection of 7th and D sts., on old U.S, #66 in Victorville, a corner too sharp and too narrow for big trucks to negotiate if it wasn't totally clear of any vehicles.

Officer Bob saw a car parked there, with the driver just walking away from it. Bob chose to be a bit cynical at that moment saying to the man, "Mister, the rear end of your car is sticking way out into the intersection." "I know," was the reply, "I can't get off the road any farther; that so and so 'No Parking' sign is in the way!"

Would he expect the Division of Highways to pay his traffic ticket, too?

Many old clunkers and otherwise illegal vehicles ply the highway from the Mexican border to San Diego. One such was a rickety old car towing an even more rickety two-wheel household type of trailer. In the back seat of the car were three goats, while three children rode in the trailer. A CHP officer stopped the outfit for illegally having passengers in the trailer, but first he was curious. "Why do you have those goats in your auto and those children in the trailer?" The old man looked into the officer's eyes, leaned forward and unexpectedly asked, "You got keeds?" "Nope," said Les.

"Aw, you don't know nothing. Those keeds smell worse than my goats!"

How can anyone argue against perfect logic?

CHAPTER TWENTY-NINE
DIFFERENT PEOPLE, DIFFERENT BEHAVIOR

Police officers are expected to act the same toward everyone, but how can they when no two people are alike? The officer may use identical words in every initial contact but receive a different response in each case. This is particularly true when inebriation is involved, especially if the inebriated party happens to be a woman. About that time the officer is almost certain to wish he was somewhere else. He knows their actions will range all the way from crying, to offering sex, or scratching, kicking, biting.

Frequently when we are giving a woman a DWI test and require her to walk a straight line she will remove her high-heel shoes, saying she can't do it while wearing them. When she fails, she frequently gets mad and beats us on the head with the high heel of the shoe she is holding. Those things can CUT!

When a woman offers sex and is refused, it is almost certain she will soon start pulling and tearing off some of her clothes, especially in the area of her chest, then yelling for all to hear that the officer did this to her and was intending to rape her. It seems a refusal is the supreme insult. One such woman did all these things to a Victorville officer who had stopped her for erratic driving, and this was while they were standing on the sidewalk beside her car. In self defense he handcuffed her arms around a power pole until he could get a matron and some help. Naturally a small crowd of people gathered around, to the further embarrassment of the officer. Sure enough, she later filed a claim of attempted rape, but luckily all this happened in front of those witnesses and the attempted lawsuit was dropped.

Another incident started with a call from a local phone asking for help. An intoxicated female was causing a disturbance. Captain Zeke Eblen sent deputy Cark McNew to accost the woman and bring her up to the old sheriff's office.

Shortly McNew was back with the lady in question, a six-foot, one-hundred and eighty pound, muscular woman. A distinctive feature about her was her eyes, one having a very severe cast which made it difficult to know who or what she might be looking at. She seemed vaguely familiar but was not a local.

However she quickly let it be known who she was. It seems that about a week before, she had become a heroine of sorts and the story, along with the photos, had been in the newspapers. In Colton she hade seen and recognized a small boy at a bus stop who earlier had been reported kidnapped in L.A.

The police were quickly notified, the man who had the child was arrested, and the news played up the story.

But sudden fame, like sudden riches, is too much for some to bear, so, for her, the reaction apparently was to go forth and celebrate her new-found fame.

All roads in those days led to Victorville, it often seemed, especially for people who wanted to drink Kentucky dry. For some years Victorville had the highest consumption of hard liquor per capita of any place in the USA.

Now she was here to drink her share but made the mistake of drinking fighting whiskey instead of loving whiskey and became a bit too belligerent for our normally tolerant citizens, so here she was, standing in the middle of the small room, facing deputies McNew and Eblen, reading them the riot act in four-letter words, all the while facing Zeke, or so the deputies thought, not knowing which eye she was using. Suddenly, without warning, she gave Carl a powerful knee kick in the groin, almost felling the man, and causing Zeke to leap backward before he, too, might catch one.

All thoughts of trying to talk her into going to her motel and staying there were abandoned. It wouldn't work!

Arrested females were always a problem. They could not be locked up here but had to be taken by a deputy and a matron to the San Bernardino County jail, thus losing the services of a deputy for a few hours on a long round trip. Only when there was no other choice would we arrest a woman. It was just one big hassle.

But this was one of those exceptions and the famous old "Shay Hotel" was about to receive an overnight guest, while a spraddle-legged deputy would be limping about. The Shays, it should be added, were a famous family who for years headed the San Bernardino County Sheriff's Office, hence the nick-name given to "their" jail.

Male drunks are equally unpredictable, and their reaction to being arrested will range from surprising meekness to extreme violence. Oddly, the oldtime hobo was almost always easygoing about it. No doubt they had been in jail so many times they knew they would have a dry place to stay, plus one or more free meals.

Then there were the tough guys who would put up a fight and would have to be handcuffed on the spot. One of these was a famous race car driver who was reenacting his racing days in the wrong place and under the influence of alcohol. When we got his arms behind his back, his wrists proved to be too big for our handcuffs. Thank heaven, he quieted down about then and we brought him to that good old sheriff's office and booked him.

Bringing in drunks who had consumed too much and were getting sick was another problem because they messed up our car's upholstery. We solved that problem to some extent by placing them in the front seat, instead of the back. If we had a partner, his job was to sit in back of the drunk and hold up the guy's head. Then, if the heaves came on, my partner would tip him forward. It was easier to clean the floor than the back seat. However, if the fellow had been wearing a hat, we would place it open end up, between his knees, and let him fill it to his heart's content. That way it was up to him to clean up his own mess. The hat was left far outside. Even the dogs would leave it alone.

Arresting drunk drivers is a necessary part of a police officer's job, and the only satisfaction for us is in knowing we removed him before he might hurt himself or others.

CHAPTER THIRTY
THE INNER FEAR SHARD BY OFFICERS' WIVES

There is an inner fear which haunts the wives of every law enforcement officer, a fear shared by all wives whose husbands are engaged in dangerous jobs.

Each day he leaves for work the wife hopes there will not be a knock on her door, with a fellow officer bringing her the news she always dreads, that her husband has been severely injured or killed. It happens all too often.

On the other hand the accident rate actually is far higher in the workplace or around home than in the obvious hazardous situations, although usually these are not as serious.

The causes behind many accidents involving police officers are quite comical. Violent incidents usually get lots of news coverage, while others less serious but equally tragic to the families get little attention, and the funny ones are only told in the squad rooms.

One of the latter type occurred when a duty officer was working at a desk while seated in a swivel chair. Without thinking, he spun about to grab something he dropped, and fell off onto the floor. He sprained his back so severely he qualified to use 4800 time off, which is officially listed as taking time off due to a job connected injury.

Still another odd accident occurred one night when a patrolman was chasing a car thief across a golf course in a footrace and stepped into a small ditch, twisting his knee severely. He couldn't return to work, the knee eventually underwent surgery, which only made the injury worse, and he was given a permanent disability retirement.

A strange twist of fate awaited him a number of years later. After leaving the patrol he went into business for himself, became very successful, sold his California firm and moved back to Oklahoma and again started a winning company. Many years later he and his wife were on a little vacation trip when an eighteen-wheeler burst through the freeway divider and hit them headon, killing both instantly.

Another accident was job related and tragic when one of our officers was killed by a fast-moving car. His wife experienced a terribly trying time as a result.

This officer had stopped a car west of Needles for speeding. Had he followed one basic principal of correct procedure the fatality might never have happened. The subject had stopped his vehicle at the edge of the pavement, but instead of parking the patrol unit at the rear and slightly to the left, our officer parked his patrol vehicle too far to the right, thus depriving himself of some protection. Or, on alighting, he should have told the driver to move entirely off the road.

In any event, the patrol vehicle normally is used to provide some protection from another car approaching from the rear and drifting toward the dangerously exposed officer.

The CHP patrolman had finished the traffic ticket and was standing by the driver's door waiting for the gentleman to sign his promise to appear, when another automobile approached from the rear, struck the stopped vehicle, grazed its side, and ground the officer between the two cars.

Soon, other officers arrived, the crash driver was arrested and searched. Not one, but two large bottles of a narcotic drug were found on him, both given to him by the Veterans Administration the day before in a nearby state. He was under the influence of drugs at the time of the accident. It seems as though druggies often are drawn toward a red light, which probably drew him toward the red light in the rear window of the patrol car.

Some justice was realized when our subject hanged himself in his jail cell.

Problems for the widow increased from the moment of the fatal collision. Among other things, her family could not arrange to have a funeral service held in his church and were refused because he had married a girl of a different faith.

As a consequence, the service was held at his graveside. To make matters worse, no seating was provided, so all mourners and the family were forced to stand in the hot sun for about forty minutes while the speakers rambled on. It must have been a terrible strain on the widow.

The casket was kept closed because the body could not be made presentable by the mortician.

Finally it was over, and the poor grieving wife had to be led away by the arm; she could not tear herself from the graveside, seemingly intent to remain there. In the limo which was to take her home, she pulled back her veil and it was then I could see the pain and suffering in her face. Shortly the sedan drew away and she leaned out the window, unable to take her eyes away from where her dead husband lay, until her car was out of sight.

I will always remember the suffering in her eyes, eyes that were trying to see her husband one more time.

There have been other funeral services for other officers, but none have touched me more deeply than did this one. I shall never forget that day.

Actually, I now dislike funeral services and and have no intention of attending another, not even my own.

Sometimes death comes from natural causes while the officer is on duty. During my career two did just that. One, a sergeant, laid down on a bench in the squad room and went into a coma. We were able to get him to a hospital, but to no avail.

Perhaps the strangest one occurred shortly after evening double up time when two of our young officers joined forces for the remainder of their shift, for safety reasons.

On this night they doubled up at nine pm, left the office, and cruised about twenty miles out when the driver heard his partner seem to wheeze a bit. He thought nothing of it until there was a second one. He looked over and saw his companion seeming to be struggling for air.

After stopping to see what was the matter and finding the officer unconscious, he turned back, radioed the dispatcher to notify the doctor, then me, and have us meet at the doctor's office. Also, she was to try to locate the wife of his partner.

Upon arriving at the medical office our officer, Fred, was placed on the examining table where the doctor did what he could. This proved to be very little. He turned to us and said Fred was dying of a severe heart attack.

We were stunned, and asked if he could be sent to the hospital in San Bernardino. "No," said the doctor, "He wouldn't live to make that eighty-mile trip."

Meanwhile a third officer had joined us in the vigil, and we acted as nurses, helping the doctor and suffering in our own way, seeing Fred slowly dying, while we felt the Angel of Death watching and waiting in the shadows.

All this took place while our dispatcher was trying to locate Fred's wife, but she was visiting out of town.

In about an hour the dying officer gasped his last breath and it was over.

There would not be any sleep for the three of us this night. We went to a nearby coffee shop and asked each other why our friend and brother officer should have to die in this manner. One thing was certain; Fred never knew he was due to have a heart attack.

Now there is a hospital in Barstow with the capabilities of intensive care and life support capable of saving life.

At least he didn't die in a patrol car at the side of the road, all alone.

The old Victorville jail. It was always unattended so no matter how sick a drunk might get, he would just have to tough it out. One drunk must have suffered delirium during the night. In the morning, when he was taken to breakfast he was insistent in a story that during the night he had seen a Japanese submarine cruising up the Mojave River, behind the jail. That was one enemy report we didn't have to investigate.

CHAPTER THIRTY-ONE
UNCOMMON DRUNKS I HAVE MET –
AND HAD TO ARREST

We often have been asked why we arrest poor old drunks. People know there are drunks, but people don't know all there is to know about drunks. Intoxication has one predictable effect, that it changes behavior, and therein lies the rub. Each person will misbehave in some peculiar way. A few will be friendly, some will be violent, but none will really know what he or she is doing at that time, and handling any kind of dangerous equipment can be deadly for them or others. For them, crossing a street can be dangerous.

Years ago we had a personable young man in Victorville who started a business with four dump trucks, hauling rock, sand, and gravel for local contractors. But he had a drinking problem. Every night he was at a bar until it closed, after which he either slept in the truck cab or he drove home.

After we had caught and arrested him a couple of times he decided to go to bars out of town.

Booze affected his work, and soon he had only three trucks, then two, then one.

Late one evening he was at a fleabitten bar a few miles away, his truck parked directly across old Highway #66. The bartender kept serving, and he kept drinking, until closing time. Then he arose from the stool but fell to the floor, whereupon he crawled out the door on his hands and knees and out into the road where he was fatally struck by a passing car. The driver had no chance to see him.

One day while returning from Cunningham's Pharmacy in Barstow, I was waiting to cross the street at the main corner when I saw a very sloppy drunk across the street, about to walk into traffic and get himself killed. I made my way to him, my uniform nice and clean, and held him back, whereupon his beltless and wet with urine pants fell down to his ankles, displaying his privates.

I had no choice but to pull up those wet clothes, trying to find a dry spot, but there was none. Then he fell down, and I had to bodily raise him up with one hand and hold up his pants with the other. Those britches had many old high water marks on them, I might add.

Now I had to half carry him back across the street, still holding up his pants, while onlookers and passersby looked and pointed. He was too drunk to mind, but I sure did. Embarrassing!

Upon our reaching the opposite sidewalk some fellows gave me a hand and we half dragged, half walked him to the jail, which fortunately was nearby.

That old boy had been on many drunks, but this easily could have been his last.

Another time I had no choice but to arrest an important man in the county for drunk driving. Because of this, and because his wife also had been drinking, we turned them over to the deputies who drove them to their home some miles away in San Bernardino.

I kept waiting for the district attorney to call for the trial, but none came. When I asked, I was put off. The case never came to trial. Some people know how to make deals.

Then we had the imported Indians from Arizona and New Mexico. It wasn't hard to see why the government had made it unlawful to sell alcohol of any kind to Indians. They simply could not handle it.

Many folks, especially among the minorities, seem to think police take some delight in putting their people in the clink for no other reason than drunkenness. The truth is, we have little choice. If we take them home, they won't stay there, or home is too far away or doesn't exist. They have to be removed for their own safety and the safety of others.

Frequently the Santa Fe Railroad would send in large crews of Indian laborers to repair or replace the tracks. The company provided old rebuilt boxcars for living quarters, parking them next to the main line. Sometimes there would be quite a few of these cars, as well as mostly young Indians to occupy them. Some seemed to have their families along.

On paydays they came into town, managed to buy liquor, walked into the alley to drink it, then staggered out. Those who were in bad shape had to be put in jail to keep them from walking into traffic, as some had done before them and would do so in the future. They just didn't show good sense.

Others tried getting back to the boxcars by walking along the railroad tracks. Some never made it.

One strange case involved a young Mexican male I came upon near Helendale, not far from a group of boxcars. He was staggering along #66 so I stopped, thinking he was drunk. Instead, one pant leg was soaked in blood, with more blood running into and out of one shoe.

He was nearly incoherent, and wouldn't show me his wound, so I put him in the car and rushed for Victorville and into Dr. Phil Lawler's office where he was hurried into a private room.

By this time the guy is too weak to protest. We were able to drop the trousers, to find the blood was coming from his penis, which had been badly slashed lengthwise.

Phil gave him a pill, the sewed up the wound, without bothering to give any further anesthetic, with the fellow gritting his teeth all the while. We had no hospital, so everything the doctor did for him was free.

Now we had a crime to investigate, not an accident. It turned out he had taken an interest in a squaw and had failed to pay for services rendered.

We had previously noted that Indian prostitutes would show up around paydays, stay a short while, then disappear until the next payday. Some of these women weren't bad looking, while some looked like they had traveled a rough road too many times. They usually arrived in pickups with their pimps. Every Indian who could afford one would own a pickup. We started calling them Navajo Station Wagons.

It developed that in the course of their drinking our subject had made a business deal with one of the ladies who, unfortunately, had failed to collect in advance, and the customer was broke. Her pimp took exception to this so he and a pal threw the lad down and proceeded to demonstrate the Indian version of "No pay, no play" with a very sharp knife.

This early day Bobbitt managed to get to the nearby highway where I found him. Had the knife been dull, his blood might have coagulated before he lost so much.

By all logic the incident should have happened during the night, but probably they all had passed out for a while. We never found out, and the deputies had more important things to investigate. The squaw entourage was long gone, anyway.

If an Indian wasn't too drunk, we'd let him go. There was no point in filling our little jail, nor did numerous arrests seem to teach them to drink less. At times our conversation would go something like this. "Have you been drinking?" Answer, "A little." Next question, on seeing a suspicious bulge in a hip pocket, "What do you have in your pocket?" Answer, "Nothing."

"Oke," the officer would say, and with that he would lightly rap the pocket with his nightstick, breaking a half pint bottle of whiskey. As the liquor ran down the man's pants the officer might say, "I guess you are right; you don't have any booze except in your shoes! Now you better go on back to camp, and don't buy any more liquor!" Do-gooders today might object to this, but that was long ago different world, and such things worked much better than the wishy-washy approach used today. Everything was straightforward, and the subject usually got the point. Remember, too, Uncle Sam passed that law, we didn't.

CHAPTER THIRTY-TWO
LAWS OF TODAY DO NOT FIT THE PROBLEMS

This final chapter is to summarize the way the laws have changed over the years, and, sadly, not for the better in most cases. No wonder crime is on the increase when the laws are so weak.

Why do I say this? The answer is simple, attorneys are in command and they write the laws. This means our laws are written by attorneys for attorneys, not for the public, though we are led to believe those laws are for our protection. Some examples will follow.

Every criminal section in every written code can be beaten in court if the accused has the money to fight it, even for failure to stop at a stop sign. This in itself means that a favorite phrase, "Equal justice under the law," used by attorneys and the courts, is a gross platitude. A poor man my go to jail; a rich man always beats the rap. An important politician probably won't even be charged for a crime he commits. For example, Ted Kennedy was never charged with anything in the Chappaquiddick death, and the investigation appeared to me to be terribly botched.

Our immigration laws should have been corrected years ago. Now we have too many illegals and their relatives living here demanding their "rights" and our politicians don't know what to do about it.

During the forties we had the right to arrest immigrants who could not show us any kind of citizenship papers or a green card which was given as a temporary permit to work in the USA. We would turn them over the Immigration Service which then would bus them back to Mexico.

There were several times when I would catch one driving a car, registered in his name (presumably), put him away, and store his car. The INS would take him back across the border, and in less than thirty days he would return to Victorville, get his vehicle out of storage and disappear. The border enforcement was futile then, and it always will be.

To make matters worse, we finally were told we could not arrest illegals unless they actually were in the act of coming across the border, because that was the way the law was written. Once they were here, they were not in the act of crossing. I never heard of that law being rewritten more sensibly. We stopped taking them into custody unless they had committed a crime.

They never carried insurance on their cars, nor do they today. We had countless hit and run accidents because of them over those years—and this goes on today.

Usually we quickly learned who the drivers were and would try to catch them before they left for parts unknown, but they had taken off for Mexico without even coming back to their living quarters to gather up personal belongings.

Our compulsory insurance law is totally worthless, as the above illustrates. The innocent victims cannot collect a dime.

At least thirty-five percent of the vehicles on our California roads are not insured. There are two options to correct this, but our lawmakers prefer to have lawsuit laws instead of sensible laws which could reduce our huge number of battles in the courts.

People look to the police for protection, but officers cannot do much for the victim until after the crime has been committed, and putting a hundred thousand more lawmen on the job won't do much good. The Los Angles riots showed only four percent of its force was on duty, and the citizens were shocked. But this is about normal for large departments because of all the days off, time off, special duties, promotions to administrative positions, and the like. In time they will retire, and that takes money.

The true weakness lies in the failure to stop criminals from choosing a career of crime. If we can't find a way to do that, we have no choice but to lock them up indefinitely, and that is expensive. It is too bad our attorneys aren't more willing to uphold the law when they know full well their client is guilty as charged. Their attitude gives us another platitude, "Innocent of the crime until proven guilty." When anyone commits a crime, he is guilty of it for the rest of his life. Being found not guilty can in no way remove the truth.

Those of us who spent our earlier years in law enforcement are, without exception, glad to be out of it today. In the early years I kept hoping the laws would improve so we could do a better job, and I listened to our legal fraternity promise the system was going to be improved but it never happened, it only got worse. Even writing speeding tickets was an exercise in futility. I felt as tho' every day I had dug a hundred yards of ditch and every night someone filled it all in. The next day I dug it out again, but in twenty-seven years the ditch remained to be dug and there were more traffic violators than ever. If I used an entire "pinch book" today, I should fill out two tomorrow.

Every aspect of law enforcement is changing. If I were to train new officers today, I certainly would train them in "street fighting." It is not an art, such as Judo, Karate, and all those other strange names, but can use parts of them. We see more and more of it because of the gangs. It is quick, fast, dirty, has no rules, and survival is paramount for the officers. Women who are faced with an attacker could put him down quickly if they knew what to do. It is ridiculous to think a hundred pound woman is capable of throwing a two hundred pound rapist over her shoulder. There is a better way.

I am not trying to teach these things; I only say they are available. I made it a point to learn something about every way I might be attacked, even to talking with fellows who had been in knife fights. I sure learned a lot.

EPILOG

Dad did not get his wish to never attend another funeral. Less than a year after the first book was published, his brilliant seventeen-year-old granddaughter, Julie, committed suicide without keeping her promise to me to talk with her grandfather.

The following month Dad's brother Rayme, died in a tragic plane crash. He was dad's hunting partner and confidant and retired as the second highest ranking person in the State Division of Forestry. No, Dad did not pass on attending these funerals and did so with grace and strength.

Dad died of prostate cancer, that nasty, nasty killer of men. Yet he did so with enduring dignity, gracious to all who visited and tended to him.

Throughout his life he loved to write. In these stories he shares his unique time and place with all of us.

- Janet -

jbthurston@hotmail.com

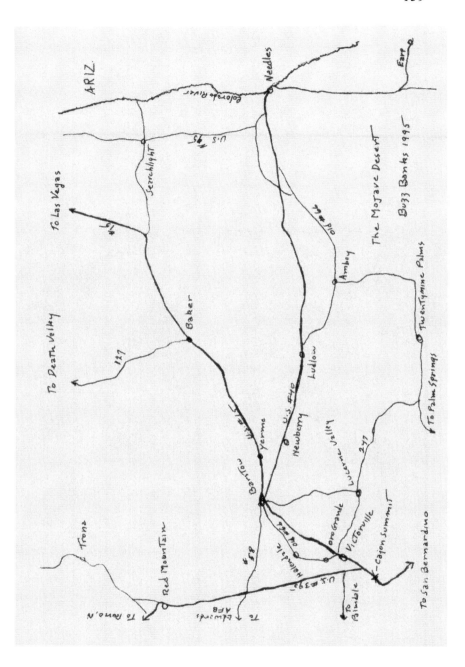

The Mojave Desert

Buzz Banks 1995

Made in the USA
Middletown, DE
18 April 2023